THE ART OF
JAPANESE BRUSH
PAINTING

THE ART
OF JAPANESE

CROWN PUBLISHERS, INC. • NEW YORK

JACK McDOWELL
AND TAKAHIKO MIKAMI

BRUSH

PAINTING

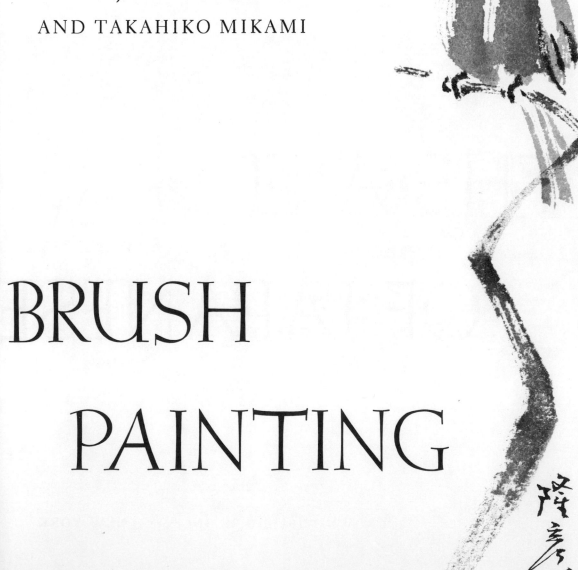

CONTENTS

PREFACE

IN AMERICA there is a current interest in things Oriental. Consider the attention given to Japanese architecture in contemporary home design, the adaptation of classical Japanese gardening in landscaping, and the special recognition afforded Japanese philosophy in the form of Zen Buddhism. With these influences, which represent a more simple existence but a fuller appreciation of life, must be included art, and in particular painting.

The style of Japanese painting known as *sumi e* is a unique art form that had its earliest beginnings in Japan during the thirteenth century. In seven hundred years it has assumed a major role in the culture of that nation and has become as symbolic of the Orient, to the Western World, as Mount Fuji itself. In seven centuries this brush painting has changed very little. It began in simplicity, it developed in simplicity, and today it continues to be the essence of simplicity. Perhaps this is why it appeals to the West. Perhaps the repose offered by its uncluttered form is now recognized and welcomed.

This book on sumi e has a twofold purpose: to teach one to extract the inherent beauty in all of nature; and to show one how to communicate the substance of that beauty in a few strokes of a brush. Any object is reducible to pure lines that depict its vitality as well as its form. Acquiring the technique of recording that vitality is the aim of instruction in this art.

Practical instruction begins in familiarizing the student with the materials—the paper, the brush, the ink stick, the ink stone—and with their proper use. Basic strokes are then learned. Certain types of brush strokes are common to many subjects; thus their mastery enables the student to recognize relationships among even diverse forms. In Japanese brush painting virtually all subjects are taken from nature. The student starts by painting subjects that have simple forms—bamboo, birds, fish—and soon becomes adept at handling more complex subjects —landscapes, buildings, the human form.

It would be almost impossible to describe in one book all of the various schools of painting that have developed in Japan, even within the limits of sumi e. Without favoring any one school we have chosen to discuss those methods of Japanese brush painting that differ significantly from American or European techniques.

We hope that this book will make available to more Americans the principles of an art whose popularity has already spread widely. We hope also that it will in some measure prove its worth by conveying the spirit of the art of Japan to the West.

Takahiko Mikami
Jack McDowell

CHAPTER 1

INTRODUCTION TO JAPANESE BRUSH PAINTING

THE BOOK

THIS IS a book about Japanese painting. Moreover, it is about a particular style of painting called *sumi e*. Sumi e (*sumi*, black ink; *e*, picture) is a form of monochromatic, or one-color, painting characterized by the artistic use of fundamental brush strokes that are based on simple lines and dots. The techniques of making these strokes, in which all colors are suggestively rendered through tones of black, are centuries old and have been handed down from one Japanese master to another. This book attempts to teach some of the methods, describes their employment in this art, and explains how they are utilized in creating a physical form whose beauty lies in its simplicity.

Why a book on painting when already there are more books on painting than could be read perhaps in a lifetime? The most significant reason is the hope that this book will stimulate self-expression —a treasure that, in this age of science and fact, is rare enough to be looked upon as an oddity. The most learned person in the civilized world or the most savage member of a barbarian society strives to transfer his likes and dislikes, his opinions, his emotions, into material form. The total of these qualities is the human character. The communication of this character to others in such a manner that the individual is revealed is successful self-expression. Generations may change, but persons who achieve this survive in what they leave behind. Since expression begins with the individual it is a personal thing. Even if it is representative of a broad cultural group, it is a personal thing. Self-expression is essential; it is good; and it is justification enough for any book that may stimulate it.

But why Japanese painting? Japan has something worthwhile to offer America through its art because it is an art that is specially characteristic of a people. Japanese art had its first beginnings more than fourteen hundred years ago as a result of the introduction of Buddhism into that country. It was natural that the first paintings and sculptures were of an ethical nature and were representative of the persuasions of the men who made them. Those earliest works of art, as well as the works of art of modern-day Japan, are therefore an essential part of the cultural development of the Japanese people. To understand that art is to understand much of the country itself. It is an art that has been shaped by a culture, and reciprocally, it is an art that has helped to shape a culture. It is an art in which moral convictions, sincerity, and a love for nature are inherent. Any one of these characteristics is worthy of consideration; together they can be of immeasurable value to Western art, as well as to Western thinking.

But why a particular form of Japanese painting? Why sumi e? Certainly in modern-day Japan paintings are done in oils, in pastels, and in many other mediums, but what chiefly distinguishes Oriental painting from Western styles of painting is the emphasis on line as a basis of technique. Because its foundation has been reduced to pure line, sumi e is perhaps the purest form of painting, and it is the simplest style of painting in execution and appearance.

Henry Bowie, whose book *On the Laws of Japanese Painting* is one of the oldest and best-known books in English on brush painting, has this to say about sumi:

The use of *sumi* is the really distinguishing feature of Japanese painting. Not only is this black color used in all water color work, but it is frequently the only color employed; and a painting thus executed, according to the laws of Japanese art, is called *sumi e* and is regarded as the highest test of the artist's skill.

Sumi e is painting in which every line and every dot is alive with meaning, and even what is not visible has meaning. Omissions are evident, and the fact and obviousness of their not-being are intentional. The beauty of sumi e lies in its plainness of color, its uncluttered lines, its simple grace and proportion. When you have experienced its animate character, and when you have mastered its techniques, you will have discovered one key to the harmony of all nature. You will have learned a common foundation of actions, affections, and emotions. A sumi painting is not a clever picture of something. A sumi painting is an interpretation of the world that will enrich our own experience if we permit ourselves to understand it.

THE ART

In an instruction book it is easy to say, "Do this, and then do that"—you learn the methods and you learn the doing, but you never know *why* you are doing what you do. This book not only presents the methods of sumi e, it also discusses the reasons, the background, the development of these methods.

Not in this art form nor in any other worthwhile endeavor are there any short cuts. There must be personal interest, and there must be perseverance. The individual who wishes to make clever pictures that will evoke the admiration of friends can gain a practical know-how by following the instructions in the latter half of the book. But the person who wants to know the meanings of the art will be rewarded by reading the early chapters. What is learned through action of the mind in the beginning will then clarify what is learned through action of the brush later. We have tried to make this an easy book to read. In presenting a brief history of Japanese art we have omitted long lists of dàtes, which would certainly have no memorable value, and long lists of names, which would in all likelihood be unpronounceable as well as insignificant. There are many fine books on the detailed history of Japanese art, and if you wish to go further into this background you should consult the works of both Western and Oriental writers. This is primarily a book of methods, but as a foundation for the methods even a few general historical facts are invaluable. As we have mentioned, past events have long ago established the theories of sumi e. Nothing is new, nothing is novel; what is done is done by inheritance.

The agelessness of sumi e is not due to embellishments of style or technique, but to the growth of what is already there. And this growth is stimulated by certain elements that are at the same time common and uncommon to Western and Eastern culture. Many of the similarities in the two cultures are attributable to dissimilarities —differences of custom, of thought, of viewpoint, as well as of place. The fact that Japanese painting is so distinctly unlike Western painting is a virtue in its favor—one that can benefit Western painting.

The uniqueness of sumi e lies principally in two of its aspects: its visual appearance and its strength of creation. The key to visual appearance, as we shall discuss in detail, is simplicity of design. Strength of creation means the feeling of the artist, or the student-artist, for the ideal brush stroke in every brush stroke. In Japanese this is called *fude no chikara*. In a painting of a tiger the power of the animal is made evident through the artist's force of expression; in a painting of a sparrow the gentleness of the bird is made believable by the artist's love of nature; in a painting of a lotus the symbolic pureness of the flower is made credible by the artist's spiritual beliefs. This is *fude no chikara*.

THE METHODS

Whereas the first part of this book treats subjectively the historical background, the differences between Eastern and Western painting, and the characteristics of sumi e, the second part deals with the tangibles of brush painting. Discussed are the actual methods and the mechanical details of using materials properly to achieve a certain goal. In harmony with the common spirit of Japanese painting the equipment, too, is simple. There are no oils, there is no canvas, there is no palette. There is the brush, the ink stick, the ink stone, and paper. If you are to paint properly you must first learn how to handle these few tools properly, for only by knowing your materials will you realize their potential. Anyone who has seen a sumi painting can appreciate the flexibility of one brush and one color in the hands of a master.

In treating the fundamental brush strokes we have begun at the beginning. That is where you should start also. And, as elementary as it seems, the beginning is a line, a dot. These strokes are the basis on which the entire structure of sumi e as an art is built, and though in the beginning they serve to train the hand and the eye, they are utilized later in myriad stylistic variations and in infinite subject applications. If there is any rule in sumi, it is *constant practice*. You must practice dots, practice lines, practice combinations of both, and practice everything you learn as you learn it.

In choosing a subject for painting you will consider—consciously at first, then, when you have become more proficient, without recognizable thought—certain factors relevant to the most effective presentation of that subject. These choice factors or criteria may be termed treatment, and they establish what will be painted and in what manner it will be presented. They, of course, are governed by the intent of the painting. As an aside, the elements of treatment are not restricted to Japanese painting alone, but are also common to Japanese architecture, landscaping, the interior design of homes, and poetry.

Deciding what is to be shown in a painting and what is to be omitted, and how the parts can best be presented to emphasize what is of greatest importance, through placement or through intentional omission—this is arrangement or proportion. Strengthening a particular effect by emphasizing one aspect of it and subordinating another—for example, making a light tone appear even lighter by placing near it a darker tone—this is contrast. Interpreting the shape or appearance of an object as it is determined by its environment or other external influences, without necessarily showing the influences themselves—the leaves of bamboo in rain look very different from the leaves of bamboo in sunlight —this is form.

What, why, and how are details, but they are essential details. All are inexorably interwoven in Japanese brush painting, and each is essential to a practical wisdom of it. An appreciation for these details, first; a desire to apply them, second; and the will to apply them, third, can result in a mastery of this art. There is nothing complicated about sumi e. Everything relating to sumi e is simple, but everything has a purpose.

CHAPTER 2

THE HERITAGE
OF JAPANESE PAINTING

To describe fully the development of all Japanese art from prehistoric time to the present day would require volumes in itself. In this chapter we have presented only the history of painting, and that principally from the viewpoint of the development of sumi e. By limiting the treatment in this way we have tried to emphasize that art modes, styles, and techniques change with the passage of years, but that despite such changes there is an evolution, a growth, of simplicity. This is a current that continues to run throughout all painting, tending to draw modern art forms the world over toward expressive clearness.

The art history of Japan, to about the beginning of the twentieth century, is most commonly presented in seven periods of development. We have described these periods as briefly as we dare. To liven the history we have preceded each discussion with a very short summary of significant happenings in other parts of the world, particularly in Europe and the near East, during these times. The perhaps unfamiliar development of Japanese culture can therefore be more easily associated with the parallel development of Western civilization.

PRE-BUDDHIST TIME

Before about 550 A.D. Japan was an isolated country, a country with virtually no definitive culture. Until then infrequent contacts had been made, through trade routes, with China, where for hundreds of years before intellectual activity had been stimulated by such men as Confucius and Mencius.

The prehistoric art of Japan before the middle of the sixth century is represented by patterns and designs that were in all likelihood created for decoration rather than for any mode of self-expression. Wavy lines portraying flowing water, or circular forms portraying flowers, were scratched on bronze bells. Regular outlines and indentations were made around the sides of pottery by pressing rope or the fingertips into the clay while it was still soft. Mirror backs and other utilitarian objects were decorated with primitive form drawings of the hunt and of scenes of everyday life. Like most primitive designs, the lines were pure and the forms highly symbolic.

THE ASUKA PERIOD (552-645)

Rome becoming the center of western Christendom; Justinian emperor of Byzantium; Church of Saint Sophia built in Constantinople; Lombards conquer northern Italy; Mohammed born, and Mohammedanism spreads throughout Syria, Egypt, and Persia.

The genesis of a true Japanese culture was in the year 552 A.D., when Buddhism was introduced from China. This gentle belief, based on individual ethical values, aroused the Japanese people by stirring intellectual activity and bringing to them an awareness of their own lack of cultural expression. Realizing their need for such elements of a more advanced civilization, the Japanese dispatched missions to China to observe and assume ideas as well as art and literature.

As seems characteristic of almost every religion or any intellectual change, this philosophy was not immediately accepted as a way of life.

For nearly forty years it was the object of a continual civil struggle between two clans, one supporting it as a much-needed cultural advance, the other opposing it as an innovation contrary to traditional beliefs. However, in 588 Buddhism was officially recognized as being "beneficial to the nation," and it was not until then that the first Buddhist temple was built. During the next three decades some forty temples, monasteries, and other religious buildings were constructed.

As has also been characteristic of the initial widening of some religions, efforts were made to disseminate the faith by instituting a religious art. Architects were invited from China to design and build temples; sculptors were commissioned to create images of Buddha; and painters were sponsored to portray, in and around the temples, representative scenes of the Enlightened One.

Rare paintings existing from this period depict events in the life of Buddha, usually shown in a clockwise sequence. The paintings are a part of the decorations executed in colored lacquer on the walls of small sanctuaries. Most of them are ornate and formally symbolic in their subject treatment. There is no perspective as we know it, no proportion; trees, mountains, and human figures all are shown the same size.

THE NARA PERIOD (645-794)

Moslem influence spreads throughout the Arab world and the western Mediterranean; Charles Martel, ruler of the Franks, defeats the Moslems at the battle of Tours; Charlemagne is born.

As a result of the Chinese-inspired culture that had evolved in Japan during the Asuka Period, and which now was growing rapidly, the Japanese government was completely reorganized on the basis of certain Chinese social principles. What had been rule by district lords became a unified, central administration. Buddhism, now firmly established as the national religion, received full support of the administration, which meant that the government itself promoted the building of temples and the creation of works of art that went into them.

As an example of the fine degree of government sponsorship that existed at this time, there was established as a major organ of the Ministry of Central Affairs a bureau of arts, made up primarily of a group of painters. These painters formed a professional staff of temple-decoration artisans, each of whose duties was highly specialized. Labor was delegated to workers who painted only backgrounds, others who added contours, and still others who laid on colors.

Many small wooden sanctuaries were built for use in private homes, and these were decorated with lacquer line drawings of Buddha and his attendants. There still was no real proportion, but the central figure of a group—most often that of Buddha—was the largest, to show its importance over the others. In emulation of Indian and Chinese architecture, murals were painted on temple walls in bright colors and in gold paste. Also, scripture texts written on scrolls were embellished with illustrations.

In addition to its principal function as a medium of religious communication, painting began to be utilized as a means of decoration. Depicted were portraits, persons occupied in everyday activities, and landscapes. In the style of the Asuka Period people and scenery had been shown idealistically, that is, symbolically flat and unreal. But now human subjects were shown turned slightly sideways rather than full face, which added a degree of realism by providing pictorial depth. Also, instead of solid colors, variations in the color tones brought into paintings a new sense of perspective. Brilliant colors continued to be used for both secular and religious pictures, but now, reverting to the simplicity of primitive drawings, there appeared the first stylistic beginnings of the use of pure lines to show form.

THE HEIAN PERIOD (794-1183)

Charlemagne crowned emperor at Rome; Norsemen settle in Iceland, discover Greenland, and reach the coast of North America; Roman Christianity continues to grow in feudal and medieval Europe; the first and second Crusades formed to free the Holy Land from Mohammedanism; Christianity made the state religion of Russia by Vladimir the Great.

Up to the end of the eighth century the Japanese government had been in full support of Buddhism, having undertaken to finance the building of temples, the copying of scriptures, and the other numerous incidentals to the spread of the faith. However, these promotional activities put such a drain on the government, so weakening it during the ninth century, that in 894 it fell under the control of a ruling aristocratic family.

In the year 894 all official missions to China were stopped, thus bringing to an end the cultural exchanges that had continued over some three hundred and fifty years. But this break did not prove to be a total loss, because once isolated from the continent Japan began to assimilate the culture it had been importing. As a result, there was formed and realized a Japanese aesthetic culture that was independently Japanese. With no further influences from other countries there developed a viewpoint of life whose accent was on beauty, and whose basis was a rich appreciation of those things, particularly in nature, that give pleasure to the senses.

Because the government was unable to continue the support of art work, the influence of Buddhism on art was somewhat diluted. Thus, with fewer restrictions on their time and talents painters were freer to extend their efforts and enlarge on their abilities by painting from nature and from life.

In the year 999 there appeared in a writing the first use of the word *yamato e*. This is a term that means, literally, Japanese painting, as distinct from *karae e*, or Chinese painting, and its significance at this point in history is that now there was a definite forming of an independent Japanese art.

The yamato e type of painting was, by and large, influenced by subjects that were closely connected with the everyday lives of the Japanese, but subjects that possessed an inherent natural beauty, such as rain, snow, mountains. Even today landscapes showing the four seasons of the year are thought of as being typically Japanese. Other types of yamato e depicted well-known Japanese localities, such as Mount Fuji or Miyajima—the shrine island—or portrayed settings for Japanese literature. These paintings were executed on small fans, on fixed wall panels in homes and in temples, on folding screens, and on picture scrolls.

Although portraits of the nobility as well as the priests were fairly common, faces were depicted without expressions, and all subjects were portrayed with a certain sameness. Scenery, too, was presented in an idealistic manner rather than as a direct copy of nature, but in a more imaginative style.

THE KAMAKURA PERIOD (1185-1333)

Jerusalem liberated by the Crusaders, but later falls again to Moslem rule; Universities of Paris and Oxford founded; Dante writes the *Divine Comedy*; commercial expansion begins in Europe, with the post-Crusade growth of towns and the establishment of trade guilds; Gothic art born; Genghis Khan leads Mongols across Asia; Magna Carta signed; Marco Polo begins his travels.

In Japan the year 1192 was marked by two significant events: the collapse of the ruling aristocracy (and the subsequent rise of a military government), and the resumption of cultural missions to China. Under the rule of a military class, warriors replaced the nobility as patrons of the arts, which resulted in an emphatic change in Japanese art from the idealism of aristocracy to the dynamism of the military mind. This energetic style was especially evident in portraiture, which departed from the nonpersonalized form of the Heian Period and began to show actual likenesses to people. And from the Sung art objects brought in from China, Japanese artists grasped the concept of realistic expression.

Many portraits and landscapes continued to be done in bright colors, but some were painted in almost monochromatic hues and others were executed in simple, representative lines that again were reminiscent of primitive forms and suggest the earliest beginnings of sumi e. Painted scrolls, now rich in motion, were popular. Pictorially they described histories of shrines or temples, biographical accounts of priests, and battles of renown. The physical shortcomings of persons were freely portrayed; warriors in battle were no longer ethereal beings, but were now active men who fought and suffered. People were shown in sorrow and in joy—common people, as well as priests and rulers.

THE MUROMACHI PERIOD (1333-1575)

The great plague sweeps Europe; Joan of Arc saves Orleans; Ivan the Great founds the Russian empire; Magellan sails around the world; Saint Peter's Church is built in Rome; Columbus discovers America; the age of the Italian Renaissance painters—Lippi, Signorelli, Botticelli, Leonardo, Michelangelo, Raphael, Titian.

The Muromachi Period was characterized by the growth of the Zen sect of Buddhism and its strong influence on Japanese painting. Zen, meaning meditation or contemplation, was of itself a philosophy of austerity, simplicity, and asceticism. It engendered a style of painting that was simple in execution and appearance. Thus came about, in Japan, the widespread use of monochromatic colors, the most acceptable color being black, because it was the purest. Here was the true birth of sumi e.

The first person to employ entirely the style of painting in a single color was an artist whose name was Moku-an Rei-en. Returning from travels through China in about the middle of the fourteenth century, he painted simple scenes that, in Zen reasoning, were thought to give clues to mental enlightenment. Later in the fourteenth century some priest-artists adapted the black monochromatic style of Moku-an to their own tastes and specialized in applying its simplicity to paintings of bamboo, orchids, and pine trees.

Probably the most famous priest-painter of this period—indeed, one of the most famous artists to this day—was Sesshu. He was first to use black monochrome for landscapes. As Ichitaro Kondo says, "The black line of Sesshu can be interpreted as the supreme art of the line and the color black, the two essentials of Japanese painting." In his landscapes he purposefully applied those principles of composition that are termed *in yo* and *ten chi jin* (see Chapter 4). Thus, in painting nature Sesshu

21

did not merely render a faithful copy of what he saw, but added a tree that was not in the original scene or omitted a structure that was there, according to what he felt was essential for a harmonious whole.

From the priest-artists and from many others of the period there originated the numerous schools that have grown in their stylistic influence and been carried down through successive years by the lineage of artist and apprentice. Interesting though the development of these individual schools and the similarity between them are, we must leave a discussion of them to a more detailed treatment of Japanese art history. Suffice it to say here that each school was known for some particular stylistic character—the choice of subject, a method of applying the paint, even a certain way of executing a given brush stroke.

THE MOMOYAMA PERIOD (1573-1614)

The Spanish Armada defeated; the Edict of Nantes grants religious freedom to the Huguenots in France; the first permanent English settlement in America, at Jamestown; Quebec founded by the French; the age of the Flemish baroque painters—Rubens, Van Dyck; the Dutch painters—Hals, Rembrandt, Vermeer; the Spanish painters—El Greco, Velasquez, Goya.

Near the end of the Muromachi Period, in 1543, Portuguese colonizers landed on the coast of Japan, and six years later Francis Xavier introduced Christianity. Thus, Japan was momentarily opened to the West through early trade, and Christianity helped to spread ideas of Western culture and civilization. However, owing to the continued feudal government by the leading military family, all contacts were quickly broken, and Japan was again isolated, this time for nearly two and a half centuries.

The warriors were still the ruling class, and the Momoyama was a period of isolationism, feudalism, and civil wars. Large castles were built for defense and for lodging of the wealthy families, and in these build-

ings the blank expanses of walls were often covered with gold leaf, then painted in rich colors. Since monochrome was usually too severe and did not brighten large room areas, black lines were used for contours and the contours were then filled in with colors.

THE EDO PERIOD (1614-1868)

The Thirty Years' War in Europe; Manhattan Island purchased from the Indians by Dutch traders; Napoleon becomes emperor of France; the industrial revolution in Europe and America; the American Revolution and the Declaration of Independence; adoption of the Constitution, the Monroe Doctrine; American Civil War; the age of the French realist painters—Daumier, Millet; the French Impressionists—Monet, Degas, Toulouse-Lautrec; the French post-Impressionists—Cézanne, Renoir, Gauguin, Van Gogh, Seurat.

Until the Edo Period Japanese painting had been art primarily for the nobles or for the warriors. The establishment of a class system had brought about isolationism and feudalism, but it also brought a diversity of culture in which the common citizen began to take an active part in cultural affairs.

In 1720 a small Dutch trading station in Nagasaki Harbor began to import European commercial goods, including books on the sciences. Japanese artists compared the lifelike illustrations in such books with their own paintings and began to adapt this personalized realism in a new art form, of which we will speak shortly.

One of the most important factors that helped to shape the development of Japanese art during this period was the variety of culture mentioned above and the consequent rise of the common citizens. These people themselves began to experiment with the arts, to paint, which meant that there were some breaks with the established schools. There was more freedom of expression, since the principle of this art was to suit the individual rather than the government or the church.

More and more, Japanese artists were assuming in their own work the realism they had discovered in the literature of the West. With art

23

becoming influenced by the tastes of the people, it became desirable to make available paintings that could be viewed and appreciated by all. The result was the Japanese wood-block print known as *ukiyo e*. In keeping with the interests of the majority, ukiyo e recorded the manners, the customs, and the habits of the people. It depicted houses, gardens, beautiful women, the stage with its most famous actors, battle scenes, fashions in dress—whatever would be of the greatest interest to the audience for whom it was intended.

Ukiyo e, because of its common subjects and its stereotyped style is often looked down on as a medium of true artistic expression. In spite of its commonality it is today perhaps the best-known representative of Japanese art: many art stores and book stores in Western countries have large selections of ukiyo e prints. And in spite of its everyday subjects it does possess a softness of color and a deepness of tone that make it outstanding as a unique art. Such familiar Western artists as Degas, Manet, Cézanne, Gauguin, and Van Gogh have looked beyond the subject matter of ukiyo e and have found there a harmony of color and a skilled balance of pure form that brought to their own work a striking beauty.

Sumi e is still a young art when it is considered in the light of the fourteen-century history of Japanese painting. As Bowie has said, "No other country in the civilized world can produce such a record." Here we have seen how the beginnings of a culture brought about the awareness of an aesthetic need, and reciprocally, how through the attempts to satisfy that need a unique art was born that fostered a culture. We have seen how this art developed, became more refined, more pure. And we have seen how certain aspects of it became an influence in other parts of the world. Can there be any doubt that the characteristic styles of sumi e are worthy of consideration and application to other modes of painting?

CHAPTER 3

THE INDIVIDUALITY
OF SUMI E

BECAUSE SUMI E is a unique art form, a discussion of the elements that make it distinctive is of obvious value. These elements are, of themselves, somewhat individual. We say "somewhat" because certain of them are phases that do appear in other art forms, but not in the same aspect that they appear in sumi e. Why is there this sort of relation and yet an inequality, particularly between Western and Eastern art? Again the answer is found in the culture of the Japanese people—a culture that makes aesthetic wisdom a basis of life.

In these pages are presented the most outstanding qualities of sumi e. It is well to remember that the points discussed not only pertain to a special art form but reveal a distinctive mode of living.

TECHNICAL DISCIPLINE

Although in olden times Japanese artists used lacquers or oil paints, they have traditionally employed water colors. In modern Japan, as in the West, there are artists who paint in oils, in casein, in pastels, and in many other mediums, but, generally speaking, water colors are more characteristic of traditional Japanese painting and are the most widely used medium today. A technical advantage of oils is that they permit a greater practical latitude; an artist can mix his colors and know exactly what tone he will obtain before even touching brush to paper, or he can paint over and thus change colors that have already been laid on. This not only gives the artist a great degree of preliminary control of the medium but allows him to correct mistakes by covering them with new paint. This, however, cannot be done with sumi: once a brush stroke has been made, any attempt to change it or paint over it will be obvious, and will diminish the aesthetic trueness of the painting. Also, the sumi artist is dealing with only black and its variants. He must therefore possess a great degree of confidence and be master of his techniques in order for his brush work to be sure and his tones absolutely true. Here there is no deceiving, no faking, and there is no excuse for poor brush work. When sumi is skillfully used, colors may actually be simulated, and delicate tones ranging from white to black may be achieved.

Another discipline concerns the matter of the artist beginning a painting and carrying it through to its completion, usually in a relatively brief period. In this regard technical skill and patience are more than traits—they are virtues to be cultivated. The latter is achieved by mastery of one's self; the former is acquired by practice.

Almost every sumi painting is executed in a single sitting, the artist not leaving his work until it is finished. Seldom is a work carried over from one day to another. To do a successful painting in this manner the artist is aided greatly by the physical simplicity of sumi e. But, as we have seen, this simplicity is an inherent characteristic. What is more important, from the standpoint of a finished painting, is the artist's reliance on his skill, his capacity to overlook trifling details and concentrate on the subject, and his emotional ability to become a part of whatever he encounters.

The reasoning behind striving to complete a painting in a short time is that the sumi artist invariably paints according to a certain emotion, a personal stirring (though his efforts do not rely solely on his being in a so-called creative mood before beginning). A feeling of high emotion toward a particular subject is transitory; it is a peak, not a plateau, and it is seldom retained for long. Consequently, with sumi e the work is done while this state of emotional stimulation is at a high pitch, because once it begins to fade it is virtually impossible to recapture.

RELIANCE ON BASIC TECHNIQUES

In learning to paint in the style of sumi e, certain fundamentals, certain basic techniques of the art, must be learned. Here is a point often criticized by persons who do not comprehend the reason behind taking first things first in a creative endeavor. Many people say, "But it isn't a true art if you have to memorize brush strokes or if you must learn to paint a certain thing one way." And they claim that by committing to memory various lines and forms a person is thereby restricting his expressive freedom.

There must be a beginning somewhere. In too many endeavors we humans do not have the patience or perseverance to start at the beginning and stay with a task unless it is immediately rewarding. Regardless of how much one appreciates the graphic arts, that appreciation will not make one an artist. Rare indeed would be a person who, on taking up a brush for the first time, could produce a painting with any communicable meaning.

Let it be understood that sumi e does not require mere memorization of a few strokes that are restricted in their application; you do learn certain basic techniques that are combined, with the aid of a great deal of practice, in infinite ways to achieve desired harmonious effects. You do not paint every tree to look like every other tree; instead you utilize marked structural differences and learn that, in shape and habit, there is a unity among all types of trees, just as there is among all types of humans. It is this species that must be mastered. When you have mastered it, you will paint trees that look like trees and humans that look like humans.

27

When painting an object, for example a camellia, the sumi e artist makes no attempt to reproduce every fine detail. Neither he nor anyone else could ever hope to do this to perfection. Rather, he first inspects the flower from all possible aspects, he touches it to acquaint his fingertips with the petals and the leaves and the stem, he enjoys its fragrance. Then, when he feels an emotional and physical familiarity with the flower, he is ready to decide what makes a camellia uniquely a camellia and nothing else. Finally, he displays that distinctive character in as few brush strokes as are needed.

This requires discipline—discipline not only of the brush, to capture an essence in a few strokes, but also of the mind, to be able to recognize the essence in every object. Thus the sumi artist paints according to his personal feelings about an object. He depends not entirely on methods, and certainly not on tricks, but on his aesthetic capabilities and judgments. Therefore, to him, expression *is* freedom.

So it is that in sumi e discipline and artistic freedom are bound closely together. There has to be discipline because the artist must see the essentials of an object and be able to set down those essentials with a minimum of strokes and a single color, black. There has to be artistic freedom because he must paint an object only as he feels it should be painted.

This emotional impressionism is perhaps *the* quality of sumi e that sets it off from any other painting of any other country. Although Japanese painting had its beginnings in China, Chinese painting began and continued in strict realism. But Japanese paintings have a much greater imaginative freedom, a result of the sensual character of the Japanese people. The artist does not copy nature. Instead, he paints according to what his senses and his mind receive from an object (this is discussed in greater detail in Chapter 4). In painting an object he displays his feelings about it and therefore expresses himself.

In any art it is unnecessary to describe a thing or a concept in its entirety. It is needless if not impossible to lay hold of all experience. No one can ever hope to attain a comprehension of all things, even in a lifetime. It is enough if we gain a true knowledge of ourselves, for no matter how much we try we can seize and express only a few moments of time. Why then should we strive intellectually to encompass all of existence in the few years we live, much less attempt to display it in written words or painted pictures? How much more practical and more meaningful a work of art is if, at first, we grasp the meaning and then communicate the significance of some everyday fact or thing that is normally taken for granted.

This sumi e is part of an inherited attitude of seeing small things, a mode of life that derives satisfaction from looking into what others usually would pass over as commonplace. To the sensitive mind nothing is commonplace. Everything on any scale is of equal importance in life and worthy of appreciation.

Perhaps the Japanese spirit of avoiding a world view can be made clear by a comparison of two pieces of poetry—one Chinese, one Japanese —that express the same thought. Here is a waterfall as described by Li Tai Po:

The sun shines upon the peak of Koro, making the mist purple;
The cascade seen in the distance looks like a long river
Rushing straight down three thousand feet:
Is it not the Milky Way falling from the Ninth Heaven?

Notice how, characteristically, the Chinese attempt to define an enormous slice of life or nature. Here is a waterfall as seen by the Japanese *haiku* poet, Bashô.

> Petals of the mountain rose
> Fall now and then,
> To the sound of the waterfall.

This is simplicity. The poet has not described the entire scene that was within his scope of perception. He has carefully chosen some little detail that stands for and defines the whole emotional content of what he experienced.

As it is with Japanese poetry, so it is with Japanese painting, and this is why, to a nonunderstanding viewer, a sumi painting may look overly plain to the point of being bare. It must be understood, however, that what is not in a painting has been left out for very good reason. If an artist is painting a bird resting on a branch of an apple tree, it is unnecessary to show the hill on which the tree grows, the mountains behind the hill, and the clouds that cover the peaks of the mountains. If what the artist perceives with the mind's eye is the bird and the apple tree he paints only the bird, arranging a branch in his painting in such a way that it will not detract from the principal subject, but enhance it. If we are painting a sparrow we must paint a sparrow and little else; if we are painting a mountain we must paint a mountain and little else. It is only in this way that we can prevent ourselves from becoming lost in

unimportant details. An object is no more complex than the viewer thinks it is.

DEPTH OF MEANING

Sumi e, like Japanese poetry, drama, religion, and music, requires something of the viewer: it requires participation. A sumi painting is incomplete because the artist has purposely omitted things. First, he does this because not all things are essential to the fullness of the subject and because that subject is increased by the omission of detail. But, second, he does this to compel the viewer to take an active part in appreciating the work. In leaving a painted scene incomplete—but incomplete only visually—the artist expects others to partake in the painting emotionally and to complete its meaning. The observer thereby becomes a participant.

For example, through sensitive observance the sumi e artist knows that bamboo in the rain looks very much different from bamboo in a strong wind. When the leaves are wet they hang limp, the stalk is curved gently, and a certain repose is implicit. But in the wind bamboo leaves point almost straight out and seem ready to be torn from the bent stalk. Thus if bamboo, and just bamboo, is shown in disarray or in repose, the attentive viewer will *know* what the conditions were when the painting was made. The mood will prevail, and this will be so without the artist having had to include flying clouds or the rain itself. The artist provides only enough so that any viewer will have to take part in a painting if he is to appreciate it fully. If the viewer sees a painting of bamboo depicted a certain way he knows that only when it rains does it look that way. Therefore it is he, not the artist, who creates the rain. The result is a simpler picture, and the viewer is more a part of the artist's work than he would be if he had merely to glance at a painting to comprehend all it said.

All of Japanese living is bound together in this appreciation of the harmony of things, and each creative effort is related to every other. In the words of R. H. Blyth: "It should be noted, once for all, that art and poetry and the drama, learning and religion, architecture and music, are far closer to one another in the East than in the West."

CHAPTER 4

THE CHARACTERISTICS OF SUMI E

INTRODUCTION

DISCUSSING IN COMMON TERMS such abstract concepts as emotional significance, spiritual expression, and symbolism is a rigorous task. In order to deal with these ideas it is necessary here first to categorize psychological "feeling" about certain things into definable characteristics—characteristics that will lend themselves to fairly independent discussion. But in treating an art whose principles resist strict definition it must be understood that categorization of ideas and qualities is at best a mechanical aid. We can no more say that in art emotion plays a role separate from that of symbolism than we can say the state of our health is entirely independent of our daily frame of mind. In either case both considerations are distinct concepts, yet neither can be intelligently viewed without at least some homage being paid to the other.

Sumi e is pureness of form; it is living simplicity expressed in painting. But in the Japanese sense of the term much more is connoted. Sumi e is a way of personal expression because a full understanding of its meanings presupposes at least some degree of understanding of oneself. Developed to the high state to which it belongs, over and above the level of being merely a novel painting technique, sumi e becomes a consistent manner of seeing life.

When the sumi artist is moved to paint he is impelled by a state of mind that calls for immediate expression. The expression lies not in how he visually sees his subject nor how he is emotionally moved by it, but in *what meaning that subject has to him in relationship to his life*, past and present. Moreover, owing to his heritage the sumi artist rises above all others by being receptive to this inspiration at all times and making it a governing principle of his life.

In sumi e we find paintings traditionally of seemingly trifling things—a tree, a fruit, a fish—common enough objects, but objects that possess great meaning for the artist. This is where the art frequently remains a source of wonder to Westerners, even after its unique practical techniques are understood and accepted. This is how its simplicity of form is its genius, and how sometimes even the absence of a form in a painting can be more meaningful than its presence. Sumi e takes away all that might possibly stand between the painter and his expression, and all that might possibly stand between that expression and the viewer. A sumi painting is intended to tell something about the meaning of the subject to the artist and the meaning of the subject the artist wishes to convey to the viewer. Essentially, then, meaning is twofold: there is the meaning that passes from subject to artist, and there is the meaning that passes from artist to viewer and utilizes the subject as a vehicle of communication. What more positive way to insure that communication than to avoid from the very beginning all stylistic impediments? Thus, the success of sumi e does not come solely from its intellectual character, but from its practical aspects as well.

MEANING AND INTENT

Emotional Significance

Mikami Sensei was once asked, "What is beautiful?" His answer was, "Nothing." Lest this reply be misinterpreted as an enigmatic oriental puzzle, a little reflection will reveal its sincerity and aptness. People commonly say a sunrise is beautiful, they say a starry night is beautiful, they say a piece of music is beautiful, but these are subjective concepts. The word beautiful, as it is commonly used, stands for a certain pleasant sensation that something arouses in us. It is freely applied to sights, sounds, tastes, even odors; any one or all, when a harmonious impression is created, is called beautiful.

But beauty is subjective, and it is relative. What creates a pleasant sensation for one person does not necessarily have the same effect on another. Some things that are pleasurable to some may be repelling to others. That is why "nothing" *is* beautiful. If a person having the outlook of sumi e declares that a camellia is beautiful he speaks only for himself, because that camellia stirs certain deep, even subconscious, associations that are unique for just that person. The sumi artist, being ever alert to discernable associations, will paint according to their dictates. But also realizing that associations more often than not lie deeply beneath awareness, he knows that without perceptive effort what he paints and how he paints is guided by his own spirit.* Creative spirit is inborn, an essential part of one's character; but just as human character differs from person to person, one has this spirit or one does not have it. If it is inborn in a person it will be there as long as he lives, even though at times it may lie dormant. If it is not inherent it can never be had. It is the presence or nonpresence of spirit that makes a creative effort either fruitfully communicable or barrenly sterile. D. T. Suzuki, one of today's greatest writers on Zen Buddhism, says: "We feel the presence [in sumi e] of a certain moving spirit, that mysteriously hovers around the lines, dots, and shades of various formations."

Beauty, then, originates from within. It is an emotional reaction. Therefore one cannot rightly tell someone else that any object or thing is beautiful, but one can—and this is what sumi e attempts to do—draw on some external thing to convey an internal emotion.

---

* In Japanese, this would be called *kokoro*. For want of a better English word we have used *spirit* to mean these subconscious associations or stirrings, which are quite distinct from emotional feelings.

It is not enough to paint in faithful copy the physical harmony as seen by the eye. What is essential is using visual handsomeness, which evokes a feeling, to create a thing of personal beauty, which expresses spirit. Feeling comes in; it is generated by something outside us. Spirit goes out; it is already within us. A lovely object, its shape, and its coloring are not important in themselves, because these produce feeling. How the sumi artist employs an object, its shape, or its coloring to convey spirit is of great importance.

So frequently do artists express feeling but not spirit. They show scenes instead of meanings. They display remarkable adeptness for technique, yet often concentrate their efforts wholly on technical feats instead of tempering them with spirit. The paintings that do display this spirit and display it to an almost universally recognizable degree, are the works of the geniuses of the Italian Renaissance—Raphael, Leonardo, Michelangelo, Botticelli. These men were obviously moved by their beliefs and believed in what they painted. It is significant and perhaps a little regrettable that, since the Renaissance, artists who have painted so convincingly, guided by spirit, have been exceedingly rare. Of late too many artists have known wide fame because of some adroitness of style or because of an ability to reproduce external appearances.

When the Japanese people view a sumi painting they do not regard apparent technical skill, but look far beyond, knowing that technique is only an instrument. They seek to discover in and behind the subject what the artist has attempted to portray, and they judge a painting on how successfully the artist's spirit shows through.

Many examples can be given of intent (working of the conscious), or of spirit (working of the subconscious), as they are evinced in sumi painting. Bamboo in wind often is expressive of familial devotion. The large sturdy stalk symbolizes strength of the father; the slender stalk is representative of the mother's gentleness and grace; the small stalk is the child—representing the artist himself, or the child of the person for whom the painting is made—flexible, yielding, yet protected by and a part of the family.

The carp is the symbol of a boy or of boyhood. In Japan the fifth of May is the boys' festival, and paper carp appear on housetops to

signify a boy or boys in the family. In sumi paintings carp are often depicted leaping up a waterfall, symbolizing the wish that a boy may be healthy and strong-willed, to be able to move not only with life's current but also against it, if need be. Thus, a painting of a carp is a most proper present to a family when a male child is born. The intent of this same type of painting may also be to intimate the striving of the artist to accomplish some difficult thing that not everyone can achieve.

Such expression of emotions in sumi e is not to be thought of as hidden meaning—nothing is meant to be hidden—but rather as underlying meaning, which supposes *purpose*. Hence the act of making sumi e, although unique in its own right, is basically not so greatly different from any other living act. There is usually no human action without some purpose. And a painting without at least acknowledged purpose by the artist is little more than a display of technique. The intent, the reasoning, the way of a painting—all are what give it living force and set it off from pure realism.

The culture of Japan is rich in the esoterics of such objects as bamboo in wind and the carp, and this explains the subject repetition in Japanese painting. Mount Fuji, a pine tree, ducks—each appears often in paintings, on lacquer boxes, in ceramics, in fabric design, and each has a depth of meaning that is familiar to all Japanese.

To Americans the eagle is representative of the United States because the eagle typifies strength of purpose, an attribute on which America is founded. To the Japanese, peace, stability, and changelessness are typified by Mount Fuji, and thus Mount Fuji has become representative of their country. Paintings of Mount Fuji are frequently presented as gifts to the emperor, to express symbolically the giver's love for his country and his faith in the emperor's competence to rule the nation.

The pine tree shows agelessness in its ability to live on for many years in spite of bending and twisting by the elements. The pine therefore symbolizes longevity and tenacity (as well as happiness), and it too is frequently the subject of paintings intended as gifts. If a picture of a gnarled, living pine is given to a person, it is a high compliment to the recipient's character and expresses the wish that he will live a long life. But if the tree is shown with a dead branch or in weak condition, it speaks ill of the thoughts of the giver. The stork and the tortoise also typify long life. Moss-covered rocks imply the living warmth and strength of the sun and signify the eternal life of nature.

Because the sun is life-giving it is believed to possess life of its own (the Japanese flag depicts the rising sun); likewise ocean waves have a vitality that is believed imparted to them by the sun and the wind. Singly or together in a painting, sun and waves signify long life. Frequently, the wish for a person to enjoy old age is also expressed in the presentation of a painting with a prawn as its subject. The depiction of the prawn is a way of saying, "May you live until you are bent with age like the prawn."

Because rice is a staple food in Japan it has become a subject that stands for prosperity. A painting may even show abstract attributes such as this: instead of depicting a wide expanse of rice fields a sumi

painter might, in a few brush strokes, portray a scarecrow, thereby indicating that a scarecrow is necessary to keep away all the birds that would be attracted to a rich crop. A turning water wheel also indicates that there is much grain to be ground and therefore a full harvest.

Just as paintings of carp are symbolic of boys, paintings of *kami bina*, or paper dolls, are symbolic of girls. When a girl is born a most appropriate gift to the family is a kami bina painting.

The subjects of sumi e have a great deal of meaning—meaning from their artist-spirit intent, which may or may not be immediately apparent to the viewer, and meaning from their symbolic intent, which to the Japanese is obvious. Sumi e substantiates the saying that one picture is worth a thousand words.

The Principle of No-action

So often in Western art action is shown directly. In Van Gogh's painting, *The Sower*, a man is sowing seed; his posture and his facial expression show determination as well as physical effort. In sumi e the tendency is to avoid direct action. First, the choice of subject to sym-

39

bolize a certain attribute usually makes it unnecessary to show effort directly. But, second, the main reasoning behind this little-known characteristic of Japanese painting is that there is enough violence and turmoil existing in life without displaying it in art.* The purpose of painting is to give to the eye and hence to the mind some degree of

---

* This applies principally to sumi e. It will be recalled that during the Kamakura and Edo Periods paintings of battles were common.

rest—again simplicity. The Japanese avoid the dramatic, the ornate, preferring to find delicate magnificence in repose.

Although there are many exceptions, the sumi painter generally does not show the excitement of persons toiling. Instead he will show an enthusiasm toward work by painting laborers going to some task, or he will show the calmness and satisfaction of having completed work by painting men and women returning from their labors. In this regard the Japanese feel a lesser understanding for Van Gogh's *Potato Eaters*, which shows people doing something, than they do for his *The Painter on His Way to Work*, which shows a person about to do something. Agitation is unnecessary to life, and anticipation becomes contentment and satisfaction.

Nature

Paintings from Japan's earliest art history dealt mainly with Buddhist subjects. In later periods—the Heian, the Kamakura—there were, typically, portraits, depictions of battles, paintings to illustrate literature, graphic personal histories. And during the Edo Period ukiyo e treated such subjects as dwellings, actors, women, and fashions in dress. Seeing how Japanese painting has taken up and recorded a variety of subjects, it is interesting to learn why sumi e deals almost entirely with nature.

The subject matter of sumi e, just as sumi e itself and so many other segments of Japanese culture—the tea ceremony, certain types of poetry, flower arrangement, and music—had its origin in Zen Buddhism. Man has created complexities that in nature are nonexistent. The keynote of Zen is simplicity of thought, of action, and of form. The trees, the animals, the rocks, the waters simply exist, growing in their own way, but bending with circumstance when necessary. Man is transitory, but nature goes on always. Is it any wonder that, to the Oriental, humanity is of minor importance? Where is the greater repose to be found—in steel and concrete cities, in machinery, or in the leaves on the trees, the clouds in the sky? This is why sumi e treats mountains and cherry blossoms, nightingales and dragonflies, waterfalls and pomegranates. Sumi e is interested in harmony, and man appears in sumi paintings only when his presence is in complete harmony with nature.

Also, virtually all of man's devices are symmetrical in design. An airplane, a building, a bridge are complete in their form, and there is no reason for any aesthetic fulfillment. Everything is there, and all is balanced. But the forms of nature are themselves imperfect, and their vigor is in their potential for completion. In sumi e the viewer is expected to participate actively in the total effect in order to fulfill the painting. Symmetry means repetition because there is equality of balance. In nature there is contrast and difference. The value of asymmetry and incompleteness is that there is always space, both physical and intellectual, for us to fit ourselves into. In so doing we complete the harmony because we have become a part of it. Thus, the human figure is more often than not omitted in sumi paintings because it is present in the participation of the viewer.

The Four Seasons

Not only is the sumi painter moved by the concord of nature, but he has great regard for the fitness of nature's ways. Nature has certain laws, laws of compatibility, by which certain objects or events occur at certain times and in certain places, and sumi e never strains these laws. For example, lemon trees do not grow on the seashore, at the water's edge, and no matter how good-looking a picture would be that showed this, the sumi artist would not think of painting it because it would be contrary to nature. Knowing nature's ways, the artist does not violate truth by painting things that are not so.

Of greatest concern to the student of sumi e is the manner in which it is influenced by the four seasons of the year and the strictness with which it remains compatible with them. If the scene is of winter, never will the artist include an iris or a maple tree in leaf; instead, in agreement with nature, the artist will depict a pine, or a plum tree, which flowers while there is yet snow. Maple leaves, but not cherry blossoms, will appear in an autumn scene. The plum tree, blooming in February, might be shown with a nightingale; persimmons, which ripen in October, might be shown with a crow.

This adherence to nature is also carried over into the displaying of sumi paintings, and to a Japanese it is inconceivable to hang a painting out of season. It would be entirely disharmonious, even in poor taste, to display an autumn painting in the spring, or a summer painting in the winter. For this reason a painting in the alcove (*tokonoma*) of a Japanese home is never allowed to remain all year round, but is changed, and others are displayed, according to the time of year or even the month. Certain subjects are characteristic of certain months —for example, the stork for January, wisteria for April, waterfalls for July, and chestnuts for October. Displaying sumi paintings in the alcove in accordance with the months brings into the home an ever-present freshness reflecting the continual change that goes on in nature.

PRACTICAL ASPECTS

Content

All objects we can perceive through our senses fall within either of two categories. One comprises all that is made by men, characterized by certain regular shapes and colors: streets, chairs, automobiles, buildings, books. The other includes all that is inherent in nature: the sky and the earth, water and air, darkness and light—that which has no definite shape, no definite color. Most Japanese painting is concerned with these no-shape, no-color things. Natural objects have relative beauty because of the ways in which they harmonize with the no-shapes. The harmony of an irregularly shaped branch is not solely in the reality of its form, but in the manner in which the branch separates the air, the manner in which it fits against the sky and divides the space surrounding it, the manner in which light and colors form themselves in it.

Here is further reason for the subject simplicity of sumi e. In a painting, that which does not appear as a deliberate stroke of the brush is just as significant, and many times more significant, than that which does. Before beginning to paint, one should spend a great deal of time looking at and into sumi paintings. The painted subjects should not merely be admired, but the *space* the subject occupies should be studied, in order to gain a feeling for no-things as well as things.

To Western eyes there is so little content in a sumi painting because Westerners are not intimately acquainted with the principle of no-things. But in sumi e one object is the principal theme, and nothing else is added unless it enhances that theme. If ten paintings by Cézanne were hung together on a wall, who could find any deep appreciation for any one of them? The eye would be drawn first to one, then to another, and concentrating on one subject to the exclusion of all others would be difficult indeed. But if nine of the paintings were taken away, the one remaining would have a richer meaning and would be longer remembered than all the other nine. There is no harmony in a hodgepodge of any kind, whether it be pictures, musical notes, or words. Better too little than too much, for when there is too much there is no room for participation.

What is the content of a sumi painting? The principal theme-object, plus the space surrounding it, and little else—and that only insofar as it strengthens the theme.

Composition

Content is concerned with *what* is in a painting. Composition is concerned with the manner in which the content is arranged, or *how* the content appears to the eye. In sumi e, as in any art worthy of the name, there are no rules as such, and we do not presume to say that content, or any other aspect of sumi e, is governed by formal precepts. There are, however, certain aesthetic principles that through centuries of application have come to be identified with Japanese arts in general, and in their association with sumi e have helped to make it the unique painting form it is. As doctrines of art they are, by and large, unfamiliar to most Western minds; as philosophical aspects of aesthetics they pervade virtually all of Japanese culture and are therefore worthy of consideration here. It would be a difficult matter to attempt an enumeration of all the distinctive principles of sumi e that relate to com-
44 position, since here again we are dealing with abstractions. For our

purposes it is sufficient to consider only two such concepts: the principle of *in yo* and the principle of *ten chi jin*.

In yo is contrast. It is common knowledge that sameness is contributory to monotony, and is responsible for uninteresting compositions. If all passages of a musical composition were similar in tone, volume, and tempo, the music would quickly become tiring to the ear. If all parts of a painting were similar—if only large objects were shown or if all objects were treated equally—the painting would have little of striking interest to the eye. We have mentioned that *how* the sumi artist employs an object, its shape, or its coloring to convey spirit is important, and also that in a painting the sumi artist depicts the main theme and little else, except that which strengthens the theme. The principle of contrast enables the artist to exploit and present his theme to its fullest potential. Thus, contrast becomes valuable in emphasizing a particular subject.

In practical terms, contrast makes the large appear larger, the dark appear darker, the high appear higher. Through in yo, compositional balance is achieved, and at the same time the import of the subject is intensified. Two mushrooms, both of the same size and shape, both standing upright, would have little interest to the eye. But if one were shown larger or smaller than the other, or if one were lying on its side, it would assume a significance because of its difference. A

mountain is large, by our terms of relative measurement, and a mountain in a painting will, by association, carry with it a certain degree of "largeness." But if a small figure is included in the picture—a hut, a boat—the scale becomes even greater, and the mountain assumes even greater proportions.

Ten chi jin means, literally, heaven, earth, and man. In many of the schools of Japanese flower arrangement this is an aesthetic principle that is utilized with great effect. It is based on the theory that all existence has three aspects—that which is of heaven (philosophical), that which is of earth (natural), and that which is of man (humane)—in this order of importance. In flower display ten chi jin is exhibited by the arrangement of blossoms or stems in the general form of an unequal-sided triangle. The highest point is heaven, the next highest point is earth, and the lowest is man.

Perhaps in a landscape a mountain may represent heaven, trees represent earth, and a bridge or a cart represent man. Although the principle of ten chi jin cannot be applied in every sumi painting, the artist does attempt to utilize it whenever the subject matter makes it practical. Even in a painting where it would seem almost impossible to depict the triangular relationship, the principle is often suggested through composition. Thus, in a painting of a loquat branch the three fruit and their placement nicely imply that relationship.

Brush Strokes

Why, in sumi e, is so much emphasis placed on brush strokes as a special element of technique? A painting is intended to convey a movement of spirit. Now if the subject is to communicate this spirit successfully, every component of the subject must carry the movement. The whole is made up of its parts, but if the whole is intended to say something, all of the parts must say the same thing. If the artist intends a painting to convey joy, every brush stroke must be made in joy; if he intends a painting to convey sadness, every stroke must be made in sadness.

In African and Indian paintings lines are used to define form, then the spaces within the lines are filled with color or tones. In Western paintings form lines seldom appear in the final work, form being shown instead by unenclosed color or toned areas. In sumi paintings pure lines alone show all that is to be shown. However, these sumi lines do not contour form—they *are* form. To avoid the limited geometric connotations of the word "line" we will, from here on, use the term "brush stroke" as embracing all marks that are made with the sumi brush, whether they are lines in the strict sense, broad ink washes, or dots.

In Western painting a variation in tonal value is accomplished by separate applications of the medium. In water-color work the paints are laid on in distinct solid areas, their combined effect providing the sense of variation, or they are applied one over another on a wet paper, the colors then flowing together. With oil paints, distinct color areas again are employed, or the paints are manually blended into one another to provide a gradation of tone to the eye. It is characteristic of virtually any familiar painting style that tone is effected by utilizing areas of the medium, and more significantly, by separate manual applications of the medium.

In sumi e, variations in tone are accomplished by certain types of brush strokes alone. Unless one has some familiarity with sumi effects and techniques, one may find it difficult to appreciate that, by taking up the ink on the brush properly and by applying the brush to the paper properly, tones ranging from black to white can be made in one stroke. The methods by which this is accomplished are discussed in detail in Part Two, but some examples here will serve as introduction to some of the effects possible through proper use of the *fude,* or sumi brush.

As seen from the side, a fish's body is dark above, near the back, lighter below, near the belly. The change from dark to light is a gradual change, and it shows the roundness of the fish as well as the characteristic fish shading. Now in sumi e the entire body of the fish is painted with but one brush stroke, and this one stroke portrays tone gradation, roundness of form, and physical motion. (This particular brush stroke is a very important one and is used in many sumi subjects. We give it the name "fish stroke.") A mountainside has many crevasses, overhangs of rock, dark depressions, and lighted surfaces. All of these must be suggested in a painting in order to maintain the true vigor and mood of nature. Here again, such diverse effects are captured by skillful manipulation of the brush in one stroke.

In sumi e there is no retouching, no painting over. Each brush stroke must be executed with certainty because once a stroke is made it cannot be recalled or changed. A sumi line is ideal because it is spontaneous and issues freely from the spirit of the artist. To be unsure of one's brush strokes is to be unsure in spirit.

CHAPTER 5

EQUIPMENT AND ITS USE

SUMI E HAD its origin in a country that possesses a great cultural richness but which has never been materially wealthy. Having been born out of a simplicity of thought and of living, sumi e grew in simplicity and was developed into a high state of self-expression by men who had neither the means nor the desire to make of it a complex art. In comparison with some art forms that require numerous implements and expensive equipment, the tools of sumi e are quite austere, and with perhaps the exception of paper, could easily be carried in a coat pocket. Because so few supplies are needed, and inasmuch as most of them can be found in the home, this is a form of painting which demands no large initial investment or continual expenditure.

These discussions of materials are reasonably comprehensive. In addition to physical descriptions we have included certain technical points wherever they seemed necessary, or where the knowledge might be of added value to the serious student of sumi e. For the latter reason there also appear descriptions of certain items that may be in common use in sumi e as it is practiced by the Japanese artist, but which are usually not readily available in America or which should not be utilized in early work.

To correlate each object with its function at once, the proper methods by which materials are used by the sumi artist are mentioned in this chapter. Their full utilization is given in greater detail in the next chapter. This introduction to them will thus establish an early acquaintance with the techniques to be discussed at greater length. We strongly advise the reader to practice these first steps—manipulating the brush, making sumi ink, and so on—in order that good habits may be formed from the beginning.

Although several types of painting surfaces are used in sumi e, the choice of a surface depends chiefly on the purpose of the final painting, not on the subject matter. However, a tradition has established certain shapes for Japanese paintings and their mountings. It will be recalled from the discussion of the development of Japanese art that early paintings were used to illustrate Buddhist scriptures, to embellish literature, and to decorate walls in temples and castles. Thus, the forms of the hanging scroll, the horizontal panel, the wall panel, and the sliding door are, even today, as traditional of Japan as sumi e itself.

SURFACES

Newsprint

Newsprint is an inexpensive paper that is used in America for practicing elementary sumi e brush strokes. It has a dull finish and an off-white color, and there are small woody fibers running through it. Newsprint is sold in large tablets (18 by 24 inches) by most art supply stores, or it can usually be purchased by the ream, cut to any size, from local stationers or printers. It is often already cut to 8½ by 11 inches, but larger sizes are better for practice work because they permit more freedom of movement. It is advisable to paint to a large scale in the beginning. Proportion is learned much more easily from large sketches than from small ones, and invariably the student finds it easier later to decrease the size of his work than to increase it.

Newsprint absorbs water well, and it is economical. Therefore it is well suited for early practice when one is learning to use materials correctly and must repeat certain strokes hundreds of times. However, once the student has advanced beyond the elementary stages of sumi e, the exclusive use of newprint should not be continued; he should work, even practice, with rice paper. It is an interesting fact that after a time newsprint becomes a psychological deterrent to progress. One knows he is using an inexpensive paper and feels that he can afford to be careless. Also, even though the cost of rice paper is a bit more, it is the most proper surface for sumi.

Rice Paper

The term rice paper is an American usage and as such would have no real meaning in Japan. There, it would be as vague a term as drawing paper is in this country. However, to avoid numerous specialized names, we shall use the term rice paper in the general sense of paper for sumi e painting.

Rice paper is the true oriental surface for brush painting and writing. It is made from plant fiber and is most commonly white, though tinted varieties are sometimes used. Rice paper is more water-absorbent than newsprint, and with the black of sumi it yields much greater oriental effects. Its surface feels soft, and it tears with a feather edge. Nearly all rice paper used for sumi work comes from Japan, where it is made by hand carefully and painstakingly by almost the same method used for centuries. Because of certain characteristics of its manufacture, sumi e rice paper has a top side and a back side; the top, or painting surface, is smoother to the eye and has less of a grain.

There are many types of rice paper, but we shall discuss only a few from the standpoint of their characteristics in regard to sumi e. The six types of greatest significance are: *toshi, gasenshi, hakushi, torinokoshi, mino-gami,* and sized *mino-gami.* The first two are of medium water absorbency; they are used principally for Japanese and Chinese calligraphy and painting. The third and fourth are very water-absorbent (for this reason they are more difficult for the beginner)

51

and are used by advanced Japanese painters. The fifth is of medium absorbency; it comes in white or a light yellow-ochre tint, and hence is used for special sumi effects. The sixth type is the one most appropriate for the Western sumi painter. It is a sized rice paper, which means it has been specially treated in order that it will take and absorb sumi well without smearing, blotting, or wrinkling.

Unfortunately, Japanese rice paper is not readily available in North America. The reader should be cautioned against using, for sumi work, water-color paper or so-called rice paper on the recommendation of well-meaning but misinformed persons. As of this writing rice paper and other sumi materials can be obtained from a few art stores in the larger cities, or through the Japanese Art Center in San Francisco.

Because its manufacture is so specialized, there are no standard dimensions to which rice paper is made. Sized mino-gami is most often used in this country, and it can be bought in sheets approximately 10½ by 15½ inches.

Rice paper in general is a thin substance, and it tends to wrinkle easily after it has been painted. When a painting has dried thoroughly —overnight will insure complete drying—the sheet should be pasted down on another, stiffer, paper with wheat paste or vegetable glue. (Details of mounting and displaying are given in Chapter 8.) Mounted rice-paper paintings should not be folded or rolled but stored flat.

There is a kind of rice paper mounted on stiff white cardboard that is called *shikishi*. In its manufacture the four edges of both the cardboard and rice paper are trimmed even, and usually a thin gold paper is pasted around the edges. It is a handsome material, the gold frame serving to emphasize the subject of the painting. It is made in various dimensions and tints, but, unless special request is made, asking for shikishi implies the standard 9½- by 10¾-inch size in white.

Silk

When the word silk is mentioned one usually thinks either of the lustrous fabric, as it appears in its refined form, or the course fibrous material, as it appears in its raw form. However, *the silk used for sumi e is neither of these*. Many Western students, eager to hurry on to advanced stages of Japanese brush work, have bought silk fabric for painting, only to find to their dismay that it very definitely does not take sumi. Silk for Japanese painting, called *e-ginu*, is woven specially for sumi work. After weaving, it is soft and flexible, but it is then sized, which stiffens it by filling the "pores" of the cloth. With e-ginu the sized, or smooth, surface should be used. Silk comes in various widths, from 1 foot to 3 feet, and in any length desired. It is more costly than rice paper.

A stretcher is used to hold silk tight for painting. Once a painting has dried it should be taken off the stretcher and mounted for display. When storing silk paintings, one should roll them and keep them in a box or tube to prevent their being crushed.

Silk paintings too are done in all sizes and treat all subjects. Silk is used for scroll paintings—both the type hung flat for viewing and the horizontal rolled scroll.

Other Surfaces

Rice paper and silk are the oriental surfaces most appropriate for the Western artist. The Japanese artist, who spends many years perfecting his work on rice paper alone, considers even silk an advanced medium and will not attempt to use it or other advanced surfaces until he is complete master of paper. Nevertheless, rice paper should not be thought of merely as a beginning material, secondary to silk. Even though rice paper is utilized first in learning the essentials of sumi e, its *proper* use requires a great deal of conscientious effort. Only through long work with both surfaces can their individual potential be realized. There are other surfaces that, although traditional of Japanese painting, are not advised for the beginning student for the very reason that they represent advanced stages of the art, and to do them justice, should not be used without long experience. For the sake of interest we mention two of these, and add that between them and rice paper and silk there is an enormous distance—a distance that is not capable of being bridged successfully in a short period.

Gold paper is made by covering a type of rice paper with a thin goldlike surface. But, unlike rice paper or silk, this lustrous medium is not water-absorbent. The sumi ink stays flat on the surface until it dries, not soaking in; therefore great mastery of the brush is required to make the strokes just the right weight. Gold-paper paintings are most often used, usually in large dimensions, on folding screens and sliding doors. Needless to say, in the West gold paper is quite expensive—another disqualification for early student use.

In ancient times artists painted scenes, sometimes life-sized, on wooden sliding doors and on ceilings in castles and temples. Such large paintings are not often done any more, but there is a type of wood painting still made in Japan. *Ema* is a picture on a five-sided board. The board is usually no more than about 8 inches from flat side to flat side, and the painting is always oriented so that a corner or peak of the board is at the top as a "roof." Ema are frequently donated as gifts to shrines, and in some shrines in Japan it is not unusual to see a wall covered with hundreds of them. The most common ema subject is a horse. The origin of this type of painting also dates back to ancient times. When a lord died, his followers would often, as

an act of respect and devotion, give his favorite horse to a shrine. But during the periods of civil wars, when there was great loss of life, the shrines were unable to keep and take care of the numerous horses given them. It therefore became the custom instead to substitute for the living animal a small wooden painting of one—certainly a more convenient scheme for both donor and recipient.

BRUSHES

In China the first true brushes were made for writing, and they were quite utilitarian. As calligraphy gradually developed into an art, a great deal of care was given to the manufacture of brushes used for special purposes. A certain type of brush might be used only for writing poetry, another type for personal letters, and still another for official documents. The design of brushes became quite ornate. Some were made with handles of carved ivory or brightly lacquered wood, and they were believed to possess a vitality of their own. Brushes made today in Japan for sumi e are a great deal less fanciful, but no less effort is put into their manufacture in order to insure an efficient painting tool. Most of them are made by hand, and only *these* brushes will give the desired results for this style of painting. Most sumi brushes have bamboo holders, and the heads are fashioned from deer, badger, or other natural hair. Because its holder is hollow, the brush is quite light, and when held correctly it has a fine balance. If a brush has a crooked holder, it should not be used. Mastering the delicate strokes of sumi e depends on perfect brush control, and a bent or twisted holder tends to deceive the hand and throw off the stroke.

A new brush usually comes with a Celluloid cap fitted over the head to protect the bristles. Once the brush has been used the cap should be discarded. Attempting to fit it back on will only bend the hairs and ruin the head. The head of a new brush is stiff from a paste that holds the bristles together. Rinsing the head in cold water and pressing it out several times will dissolve the paste and soften the bristles. It is very important that brushes be washed thoroughly after each painting session to clean out all sumi and keep the hairs soft. A

55

brush must never be put in hot water; hot water spoils the flexibility and loosens the hairs. The best way to protect a brush when it is not in use or when it is being carried is to keep it rolled up tightly in a section of tied bamboo strips, which can be cut from a bamboo place mat.

Although there are many types of painting brushes manufactured in the United States, and even though many of them are called "Japanese," they are *not* Japanese brushes and they cannot be used for sumi e. The only brush for Japanese painting is made in Japan. The people who make them are guided by centuries of experience and know just how many hairs should be used, how stiff or soft they should be, how to tie them, and how to join them to the holder. It is very important not to use a Chinese or Japanese writing brush for painting. A writing brush has neither the correct balance nor the proper suppleness for proper use in sumi e. And more significant, a writing brush is made to be wet normally only at the tip. If such a brush is immersed completely in water, as must be done with sumi e, the glue holding the bristles to the handle may dissolve and the entire head may drop off!

Especially with brushes, there should be no compromise with quality. Even the beginner should beware of cheating himself by using inferior equipment. The brush is the tool that translates the artist's mental intent into recognizable forms. It is the most intimate connection between the artist's mind and his painting. In sumi e the brush is all-important.

There are two principal types of brush used for sumi e. The *fude* has a round but sharply pointed head that is quite flexible when wet. Its holder is usually bamboo, about 8 or 9 inches long (an inch or two longer than a writing brush). The fude is the most often-used brush, the very tip being utilized for thin lines and dots and the entire width of the head for strong, wide strokes. The *hake* is a flat brush, made in sizes from 1 inch to 4 or more inches wide. It is used for adding washes, or for laying on a foundation of sumi when the area to be covered is such that the fude could not give an over-all even tone. Both types are made in small, medium, and large sizes. The student should use the medium or even small size. Large sumi brushes *are* large—a

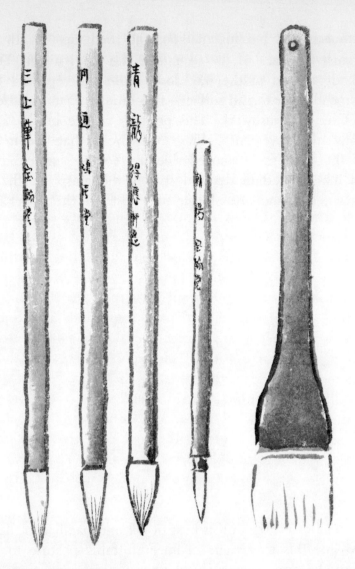

large hake looks like a housepainter's brush—and are used for big scrolls, folding screens, or larger areas.

After several month's use the tip of a fude will become worn, and will no longer be usable for painting fine lines. Such a brush should not be discarded, but should be saved for making wide lines or heavy strokes.

The fude is not grasped as is a pencil, tucked in the root of the thumb and forefinger and slanted to the painting surface, but is held

57

between thumb and forefinger, almost at their tips, so that it rests lightly against the back of the second or the third finger. The fingers remain about a third of the way down from the top, and the brush is kept perpendicular to the surface—a technique characteristic of Japanese and Chinese brushwork. This position of the brush is sustained for virtually all movements other than those that require the full length of the head to be moved sideways to the surface for a wide stroke. In making certain detailed strokes the grasp on the brush is moved down, and the little finger may rest on the paper to steady

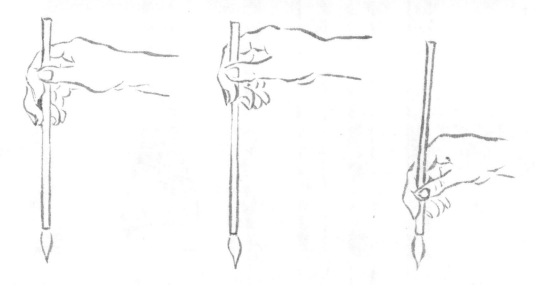

the hand. In all cases, the arm is kept up off and parallel to the painting surface. At first this may seem an uncomfortable posture to maintain, and because the arm is in such an unaccustomed position, the early strokes may be unsteady. By conscientious practice, not permitting the elbow to rest on the table, the student will soon realize great control over his muscles and the brush, and much more freedom of movement.

SUMI

To the viewer of a Japanese painting the only visible impression of the artist, his efforts, and his techniques is that given him by the sumi, or painted color. To a viewer, years after a painting has been made, the artist is no longer an actual being, his brush has long ceased to have reality, and the surface itself seems to be nonexistent. All that remains is the *spirit* of the artist, kept constantly alive by the lines and dots of sumi. Sumi is the living record of the painter. In new paintings brush strokes are fresh and stand out boldly against their background. On an old painting, even though the surface may be brown and cracked with age, the sumi mellows with the years, takes on a quiet softness, and continues to live.

Sumi is not a true ink, though that term is often used in referring to it, and it is not a paint in the common sense of the word. It is easier to say what sumi is not than what it is. At best, we can define it as a sort of black water color. Sumi is sumi. It is what makes Japanese paintings unique in the arts. Sumi is usually black, though some special types have a light bluish or brownish cast. Some types are scented, and some have gold flakes in them, but neither of these embellishments can make a bad painting any better.

Sumi is made in a rectangular cake, usually about the size of a package of chewing gum, by solidifying a mixture of carbon and glue and pressing the mixture into a block. In China, ink sticks were used in writing as early as the seventh century A.D., and in Japan sumi has been used in writing and painting for almost as long. The sumi stick often has a design or lettering pressed into it, telling the name of the manufacturer or the type of sumi.

59

One or both ends of a sumi stick are square and flat. In making ink the stick, held perpendicular to the wet ink stone with the flat end down, is rubbed gently on the stone until a thick ink is formed. The stick must not be rocked or tilted, since this will wear an uneven surface and make the grinding of good ink more difficult. Even this is a technique that must be learned properly. In Japan, when an apprentice goes to a master to learn painting, one of the earliest tasks given him is that of making ink. There are more wrong ways of doing this seemingly simple chore than there are right ways, and after several months of doing nothing but rubbing a sumi stick, an apprentice will have indicated to the master whether he has the perseverance and patience necessary to become a painter.

SUZURI

The *suzuri* is the ink-grinding stone. Some suzuri are made by molding and baking river clay, but the best Japanese ink stones are cut from a black rock, similar to slate, found near Hiroshima on the island of Honshu. Most suzuri are rectangular in shape, measure about 3 inches by 5 inches, and are about ½ inch thick. The top of the suzuri is depressed slightly to a flat grinding surface called the land, on which the sumi stick is rubbed when making ink and from which the ink is taken up with the brush. At one end of the stone the land slants

down to a well called the sea, which, prior to grinding ink, is filled half-way with water. The suzuri is always placed with the sea away from the artist. Sumi should never be ground on any surface other than the suzuri. After every painting session the suzuri should be washed thoroughly with cold water to prevent old sumi from drying and caking on it.

MISCELLANEOUS EQUIPMENT

The *fude-arai* is the water well. It holds water for thinning sumi ink on the fude or for washing out the fude. A fude-arai is made of china or metal, and has compartments, but any deep dish, cup, or jar will serve as a water well.

The *sara* is a small white dish used as a palette for testing the color of sumi on the brush. In Japan some sara are made in delicate flower shapes; others comprise a set of dishes that are sometimes made to nest into one another. A shallow white saucer with a glazed surface makes a very good sara.

Very often too much ink or too much water is taken up on the brush and the excess must be blotted out. For this a piece of white cotton material folded into a pad (*fude-fuki*) is used.

61

Fude, sumi, suzuri, fude-arai, sara, and fude-fuki are basic. There are many other tools used by the Japanese artist, special tools that are useful but not absolutely essential for the student. A brush rest, or *fude-oki*, keeps wet brushes off the table when more than one brush is used. Fude-oki are made of china, bamboo, or carved wood, and they often appear in such interesting forms as a fish, an arched bridge, a dragon. The *fude-maki* is a brush carrier, made of thin strips of bamboo held together with interwoven threads, in which the sumi brush is rolled. An oriental place mat, or a section of bamboo window blind, makes an excellent fude-maki. *Shitajiki* is a large piece of thick felt that is spread out on the painting table and on which the paper is placed for painting. The felt protects the table from sumi stains, and lets the paper yield to the brush.

Although rice paper is placed flat, silk cannot be allowed to touch any surface while it is being painted on. A silk stretcher is a simple rectangular wooden frame that can easily be constructed by the student, and it holds silk taut until the painting is dry. Its dimensions should be slightly less than the dimensions of the silk to be mounted, and the corners of the frame should be braced so that it will keep its shape. When stretching silk, pull it taut on the frame and tack the four corners down. Then brush wheat paste or vegetable glue around the edges of the silk, and secure them to the frame. No paste must drop on the painting surface, and brush strokes must not reach the edge of the silk or the water will loosen the paste.

CHAPTER 6

BASIC LINES AND STROKES

BEFORE ANY BRUSH STROKE is made the sumi artist must make several
decisions governed by the subject to be painted and thus by the part
played by a particular line. In the early steps of learning, these decisions
are reached consciously; as familiarity with the techniques grows, they
are automatic. First the artist must decide on the thickness of the ink
to be taken up on the brush. The brush will be inked lightly (almost
dry), moderately, or heavily (wet), depending on the purpose of the
stroke and also on the length of line to be painted. If either a wet-look-
ing stroke or a long, continuous line, solid from start to finish, is desired,
the brush must be inked heavily. In general, a dark, rich-looking stroke
is made with a wet brush containing thick ink. A light, even-tone stroke is
made with either a wet or a medium brush containing thin ink. If a
line is intended to show alternate light and dark areas, to indicate a
special form (such as a bamboo trunk), the brush must be "dry." For
a dark line that breaks up along its length into white patches, the brush
is inked lightly, but with thick ink—the dry patches on the paper contrast strikingly with the dark-ink areas. A light line that breaks up into
patches is made with a dry brush inked lightly. In such a line the patches
blend rather than contrast with the light-ink areas.

Next, the artist must decide how the brush is to be oriented with respect to the painting surface. Should the brush be perpendicular to the surface, slanted slightly, or slanted greatly? Here the answer is not governed solely by the tone gradation desired in a certain line: the shading can vary, not only from one orientation to another, but also within the same orientation, depending on the inking of the brush. To say that the brush must be slanted is not enough, since different lines are produced by slanting it toward the body, away from the body, or to either side. Again, the answer is in the purpose of the stroke. For example, a dry brush and a slightly side-slanted stroke are used in making

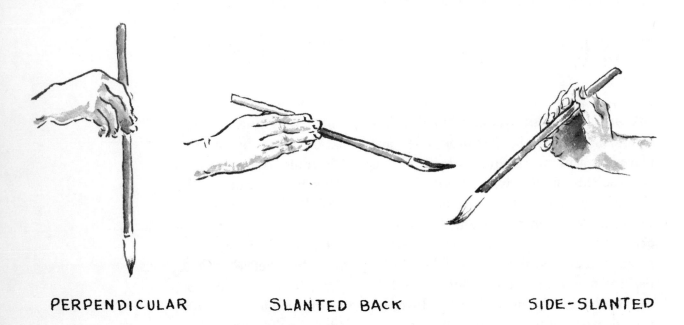

PERPENDICULAR   SLANTED BACK   SIDE-SLANTED

rocks or rocky mountains; a wet brush and a greatly side-slanted brush are used in making a large tree trunk; a moderately wet brush and a back-slanted stroke are used for the fish shading.

The position of the ink *on the brush head* is a very important consideration. A brush inked only at the tip produces one kind of line; a brush inked higher than the tip, with the tip dry or lightly inked, produces a different line. Some strokes require the end of the brush to be

64

pointed, whereas others require it to be flattened or spread out like the open hand. All of these factors are treated in the exercises in this chapter and in the lessons in Chapter 7. It is imperative that the instructions for each stroke be followed closely until confidence is gained in brush technique. Then you may vary the dryness or wetness of the brush for different orientations and different thicknesses of ink, and investigate the great potentialities of the sumi tools.

We have already spoken of spirit in regard to the artist's "feeling" toward his subject. Every line, every mark, made by the brush on the painting surface must be made with full spirit if it is to add meaning to the over-all picture. In making a stroke the artist must think of the function of that stroke, as it relates to the total subject, from its beginning to its end. For example, while a line depicting a plum branch is being made, the mind must visualize nothing but the plum branch. As the line grows, the mind projects itself into the branch and experiences growth. To carry the example further, both feet should be firmly on the ground and should be thought of as being rooted in the earth. The legs should be thought of as the trunk of the tree, the arms as branches. The spirit will then seem to flow from the ground, up through the body, and out through the fingers into the sumi brush. The brush should not be consciously forced by the hand or the fingers, but should be guided smoothly by this flow of spirit. Since sumi e is an art of tranquility, the surroundings of the artist as he works must be tranquil. Distracting loud music or conversation tend to weaken the effects of the spirit because they do not permit the artist to concentrate.

In olden days, when sumi e was even more of a spiritual endeavor than it is now, an artist might go to the mountains to obtain pure spring water for a painting. Many of the old masters arose early in the morning to draw the first water from the well. Although such noble practices are not essential to good sumi painting, clean water is. Discolored water must never be used. Also, the brush should not be used to transfer water from the fude-arai to the suzuri; instead, a small amount of water is poured from the fude-arai into the sea of the suzuri.

Try to work at a table that is lower than a normal writing desk, since this allows the eyes to look straight down at the surface instead

of viewing it at an angle. Place all equipment—fude, sumi, suzuri, fude-arai, fude-fuki, sara—to your right (to your left if you are left-handed). Rest the left hand on or near the painting surface to balance your body. Using newsprint in the beginning, or until you feel adept enough to try rice paper, place the surface straight, directly in front of you. Never move the surface while painting—move only the brush or your body. Tilting the surface destroys visual balance and thus the composition.

Dip the flat end of the sumi stick into the water of the suzuri sea, and keeping the stick on the stone's surface, slide it up out of the sea toward you, onto the land, drawing some water with it. Repeat this several times until the land is wet. Then, holding the sumi stick perpendicular to the land, rub it gently in an oval, with a "round" (peaceful) mind. (An artist who tips his sumi stick when rubbing ink is said to be "crooked-minded.") Always make a thick ink on the land; that is, don't try to fill the sea with thick ink. The sea is a water reservoir,

66

and the land is a holder for the ink. To darken the ink on the brush, pick up thick ink from the land on the brush tip; to lighten or thin the ink on the brush, dip it into the sea. Touch the brush on the edge of the sara to test the ink. If it is still too dark, dip the tip of the brush into the sea and again test it on the sara. If the brush has too much water, wipe it on the fude-fuki toward you, to keep the tip pointed.

In the following exercises, and in the lessons in Chapter 7, repeat each subject according to the detailed instructions, until you are able to make all of the strokes and lines the way they are shown. To most Westerners Japanese brush painting is altogether new and its techniques are unfamiliar and uncomfortable, so do not become discouraged if the brush positions seem awkward or the lines are difficult to make. You cannot repeat these fundamental strokes too frequently. Follow the numbers for the proper order of making the strokes, and make them in the directions indicated. These exercises and lessons have evolved from many years of teaching Americans. The strokes, their order, and their direction may not always be the same as those done by Japanese sumi artists, but they seem to be the best suited for Americans. Always master one page of instruction before going on to the next, even if the mastery takes several sessions. Once a lesson is learned, do not forget it; from time to time, even when you are in the advanced subjects of Chapter 7, return to these basic exercises and review the lines and strokes.

Dots

Bird eye (just press)

Other examples of bird eye

Beak

Pine cone

Feather (flat brush)

Grain

Tree

Deer hoof

Press

Brush slanted

Pine

Wisteria petal

Flower petal

Brush straight up

Leaves

Mushroom head

Narrow leaves

Lines and Strokes

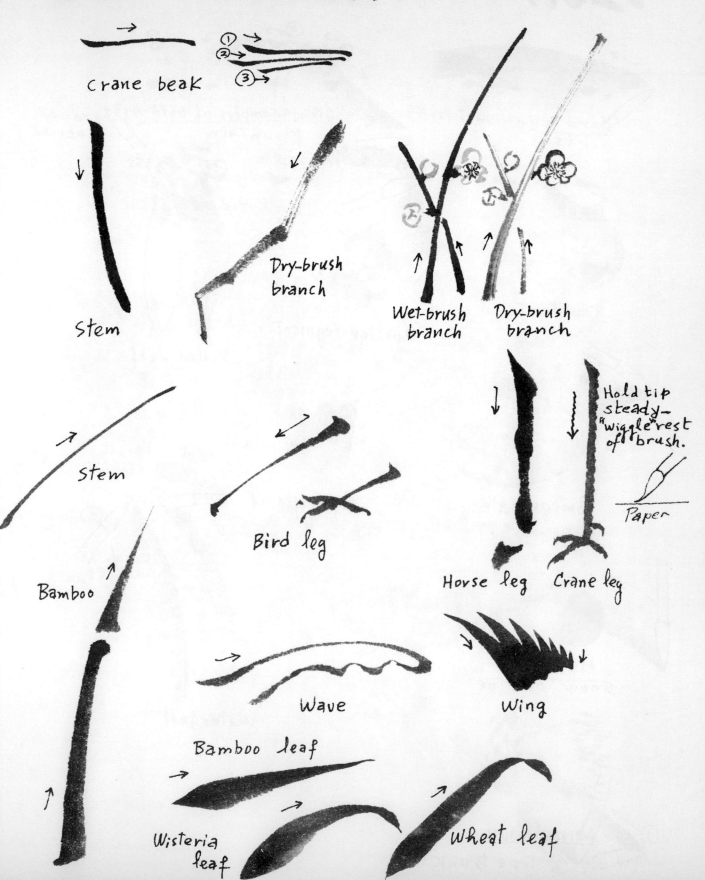

crane beak

① → ② → ③ →

Stem

Dry-brush branch

Wet-brush branch

Dry-brush branch

Stem

Bird leg

Hold tip steady— "wiggle" rest of brush.

Paper

Horse leg   Crane leg

Bamboo

Wave

Wing

Bamboo leaf

Wisteria leaf

Wheat leaf

Shaded strokes

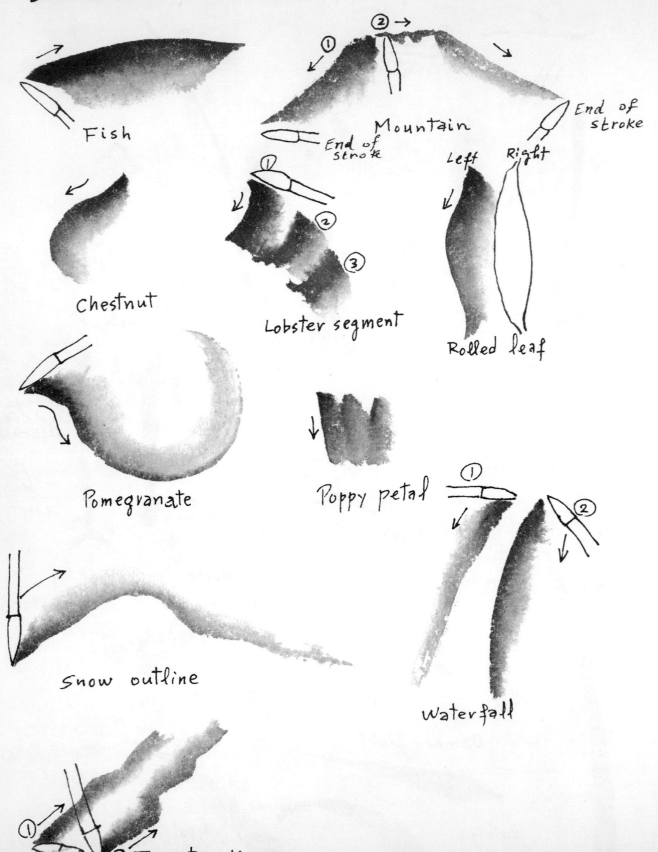

Fish

Mountain

② →

① End of stroke

End of stroke

Left   Right

Rolled leaf

Chestnut

① ② ③

Lobster segment

Pomegranate

Poppy petal

① ②

Waterfall

Snow outline

① ② Tree trunk

Slanted brush

Leaf

Leaf

Petal

Pressing

Maple leaf

Flower

Leaf

Tail fin

Chrysanthemum
leaf

Make in three strokes:

(1) Center
(2) Left lobes
(3) Right lobes

Press heel
of brush for
first lobe, then raise heel but
not tip, then press heel again
for second lobe.

Side of brush

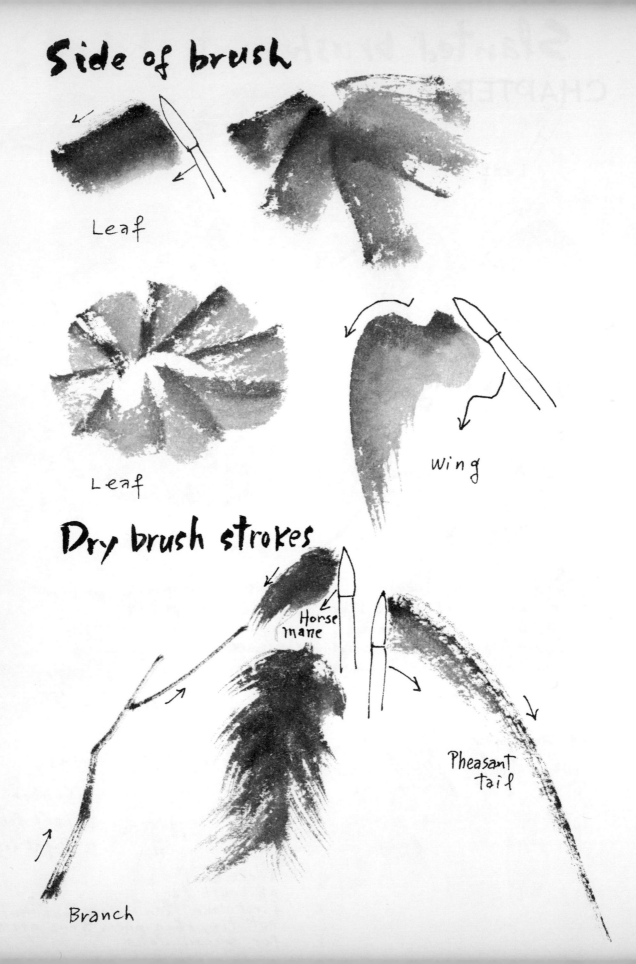

Leaf

Leaf

Wing

Dry brush strokes

Horse mane

Pheasant tail

Branch

CHAPTER 7

THE PAINTING

ALMOST ALL of the subjects given as sumi lessons in this book deal with nature. We have included some subjects, familiar to the Westerner, which are not strictly Japanese in their aspect. However, it is not entirely the subject that makes a sumi painting look Japanese—not every painting has to contain bamboo or a moon bridge. What is more important than subject is treatment and technical discipline. On the other hand, some of the subjects may be so unfamiliar as to seem strange. The majority of these have been included because they are strongly Japanese in their aspect and because they illustrate some principle, for example ten chi jin or in yo.

Each subject combines old and new strokes in different ways, so do not skip over any subject. Even though you may not like flowers, for example, or horses, discipline yourself to master each subject in turn before going on to the next. What you learn in one lesson will be used in another, and although the strokes may be modified, their basic character must be learned. A stroke that makes a mountain slope in one painting may make the neck of a goose in another painting. When you begin a new subject concentrate first on the individual brush strokes, striving by practice to perfect each one. Follow the instructions closely. Then when you gain confidence, and your strokes look like those given, think of a subject as a whole, and permit your spirit to take over. Trying to force your spirit to control the brush before *you* can handle it will result only in failure.

Make your paintings the same size as those in the lessons. Later, if you wish, you can paint to a larger scale, but do not paint to a smaller scale. Sumi e, to realize its full purpose, must not be done small. Miniature oriental paintings have been either photographically reduced or are a product of a style other than sumi e. When a subject has been mastered as it is given here, an excellent discipline is to teach yourself to paint the same subject in reverse. For example, the painting of a heron facing the left should be done to show the heron facing the right. If you are left-handed and are having trouble with a particular subject, reversing it will usually help.

Your early efforts may look odd, not at all like the paintings in the book. No matter how awkward they may seem or how far out of proportion they may be, *never* attempt to touch up the strokes. This cannot be done in sumi e. In your learning, the strokes themselves are much more important than the proportion, or the shape, or even the over-all composition.

When you have mastered all the subjects given here, and when you feel that not your hand but your spirit is controlling the brush, choose your own subjects from nature. Select animals peculiar to your geographic region, or landscapes you are familiar with. Study them, and mentally reduce them to their essential forms. Gain a feeling for them—with your spirit achieve a personal kinship. Then apply what you have learned about sumi e to create your own paintings.

74

Together with pine and bamboo,
the plum tree is one of the
three trees symbolizing HAPPINESS.
The three combined are often
used for auspicious occasions.

(1) Trunk and branches first
All strokes from bottom to top.
Medium color.

梅

Plum-tree

(2) Blossoms

Dots on trunk in
dark color.
These dots show
moss which has
grown on the tree,
showing it is an
old one.

Another way is to
draw each petal
with two strokes.

枇杷
Loquat

(1) Fruit and branch first

(2) Leaves next

(3) Veins
Use brush straight up with dark, thick ink.

① Dark color: use side of brush.
② Medium tone: dry brush; use side of brush.
③④ Medium tone: wet brush; use brush almost straight up.
⑤ Light color: wet brush.
⑥ Medium tone: moderate amount of moisture.

Dark color is only for the *first* touches for grains, also veins on leaves.

wheat

(1) Grains first

Dots from top to bottom starting from the left.

(2) Ears next

From bottom to top.
Tip of each ear should be pressed gently.

↑ **Do Press.**

↑ **Don't lift.**

(3) Stem
From top to bottom.

(4) Leaves
From bottom to top in one stroke each.

Hold brush straight up.

↗

Draw veins with dark, thick ink.

椿

Camellia

(1) Flower - light color

Stamens first.
(Dots on top are dark.)
Draw outlines for petals with slow speed, brush straight up.

Calyx -
slant brush

(2) Bud

(e)

(c)

(d)

(3) Branch from bottom to top with dark color.

(a)

(4) Leaves
Draw in order of (a), (b), (c), (d), (e).

Leaf (a)

(b)

This is an example of the suggestion of time and place with the help of secondary subjects.

The reed suggests WHEN and WHERE the goose comes.

Reeds grow near water, and flowers of the reed indicate late autumn, as they are withered and bent.

飛雁

Flying goose

(1) Beak, eye, and jaw
(2) Head, neck, and body
(3) Wings

(4) Tail, feet, and fine feathers on body

Open tip of brush.

(5) Reed

Wisteria

藤花

(1) Blossoms
Wet brush, applying ink to half of brush.

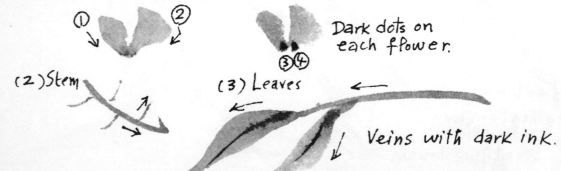

① ②

Dark dots on each flower.

③④

(2) Stem

(3) Leaves

Veins with dark ink.

(4) Vines with medium and dark ink

Simplified method of drawing birds

Beak, eye, and head

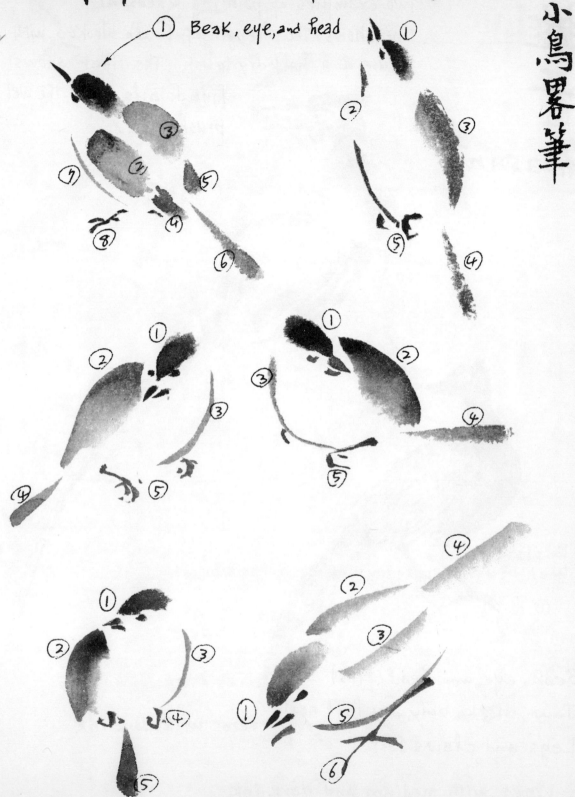

小鳥畧筆

雉子

Pheasant

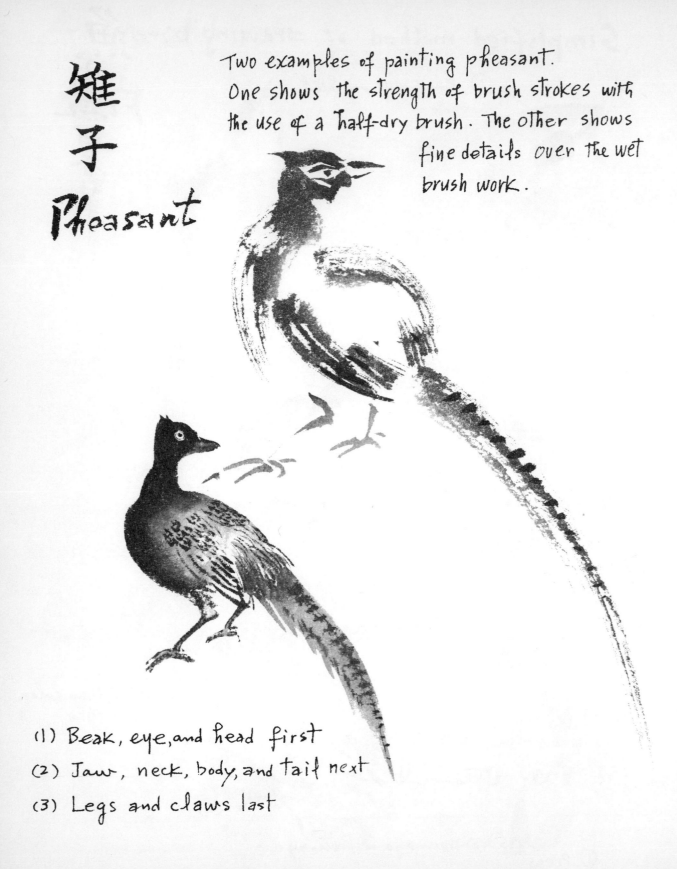

Two examples of painting pheasant. One shows the strength of brush strokes with the use of a half-dry brush. The other shows fine details over the wet brush work.

(1) Beak, eye, and head first

(2) Jaw, neck, body, and tail next

(3) Legs and claws last

魚
Fish

(1) Wash brush with clean water, remove excess water.
Apply dark ink only at tip of brush.

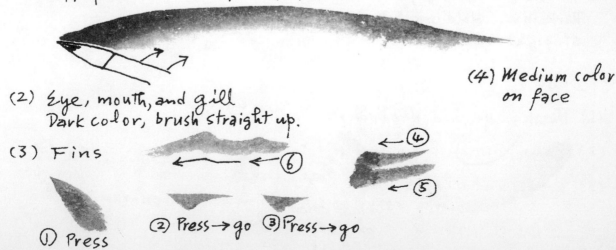

(2) Eye, mouth, and gill
Dark color, brush straight up.

(3) Fins

(4) Medium color
on face

← ④

← ⑥

← ⑤

① Press   ② Press → go   ③ Press → go

金
魚 **Goldfish**

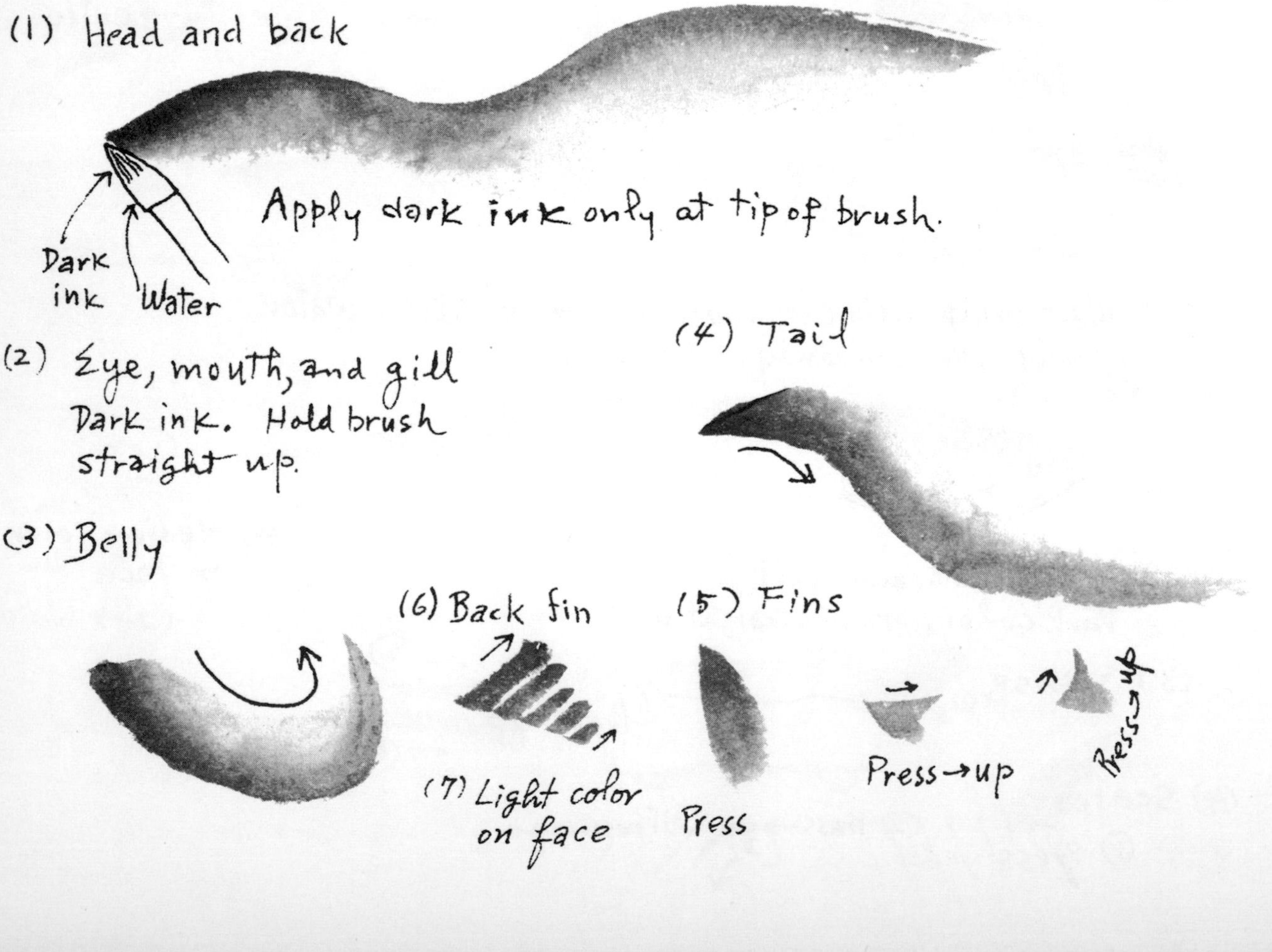

(1) Head and back

Dark ink   Water

Apply dark ink only at tip of brush.

(2) Eye, mouth, and gill
Dark ink. Hold brush
straight up.

(3) Belly

(4) Tail

(6) Back fin

(5) Fins

(7) Light color
on face

Press

Press→up

Press→up

鯉
Carp

The carp plays a unique part in the Japanese garden. Many of the old Japanese gardens have ponds in which there are many carp in a great range of color: gold, pink, red, black, white with red spots, etc. The movement of groups of carp in a pond gives a gentle accent to the quiet Japanese garden.

(1) Head and back

Dark ink

Water

(2) Eye, mouth, gill

(3) Fins

Press

Press-up

(4) Scales

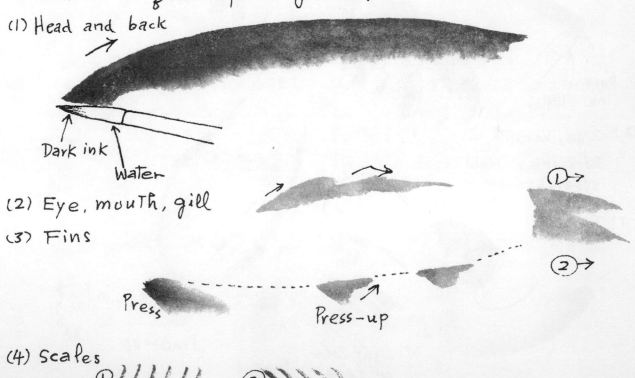

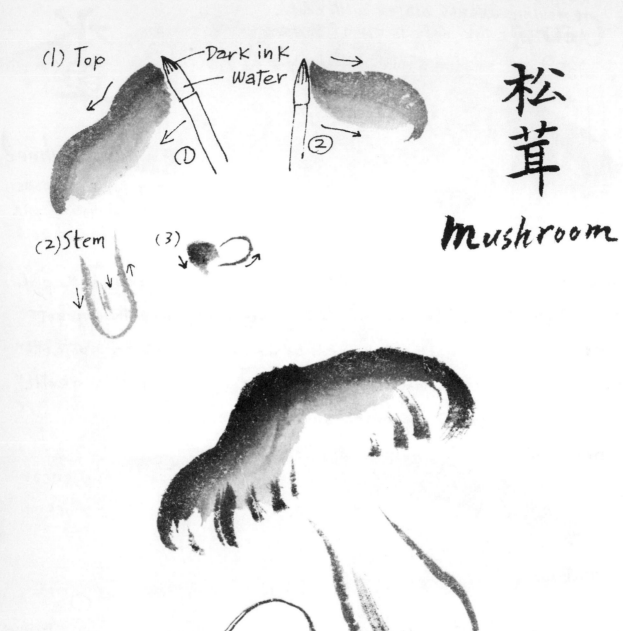

(1) Top

Dark ink

Water

①

②

松茸

Mushroom

(2) Stem

(3)

(1) Shaded strokes to show snow.
Wash brush with clean water,
removing excess water with cloth.
Apply dark ink only to tip of brush.
Paint all shaded stroke outlines.

水車

Water wheel

This picture shows
a farm house with
its water wheel
attached.

The stable is built
right in the house.

In modern Japan
it is not too easy
to find this type
of
house near
large cities.

When not covered with snow

(2) Dark-color ink for
other parts

(1) Cormorant
Wash brush, remove excess water
from tip, and apply dark ink to
half of brush.

鵜
Cormorant

One
stroke

Use brush straight up,
start from end of beak
to bottom of neck, then
slant brush for body.
Outline left side of
body with light color.

(2) Land
Dark ink from right to left, slanted brush.

(3) Reeds with medium color

(4) Moon   Medium ink on tip of brush,
as in snow outline.

Mt. Fuji is the highest and most beautiful mountain in Japan and is the symbol of peace of the nation.

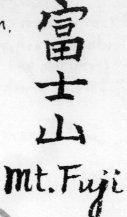

富士山
Mt. Fuji

(A) OUTLINES

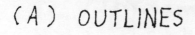

(1) For outline of the mountain hold brush straight up, and draw with medium-color ink.

(2) Light-color touches on the mountain, then dark-color touches over them.

(B) SHADED STROKES

(1) Shaded stroke on left side first, then top and right side.

(2) For shading on the mountain use side of brush. Light color first, darker tone later. Strokes from bottom to top.

Here are some classic examples of bamboo leaves and nodes
which were first introduced to Japan from China many hundreds of

WITH
DEW

years ago. These "fixed styles" are still considered very
valuable, important, and necessary for study for any one

IN
WIND

pursuing this type of painting. I heartily agree. However,

ON
FINE
DAY

as art is something which is created by the artist, it is not

IN
RAIN

necessary to adhere to them when you paint with your own

NODES

feeling and idea.

EXAMPLES OF LEAVES ON STEM

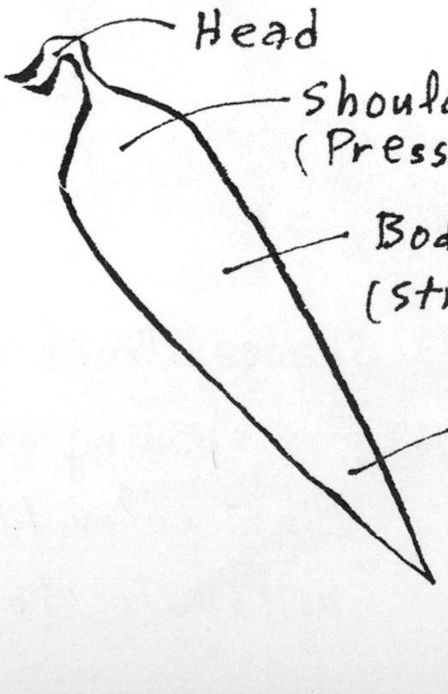

Head
Shoulder
(Press)
Body
(straight)
Tail
(sharp)

The bamboo is one of the three trees which symbolizes happiness — the others, the pine and the plum.

竹

Bamboo

(1) Branches first
Use brush straight up. Draw from bottom to top.
(2) Leaves

風
竹

Bamboo in wind

(1) Medium-color ink for branch and stems.
Hold brush straight up.
Draw from bottom to top, just as the bamboo itself
grows.
Nodes with dark color.
(2) Left-side leaves — dark color.
Right-side leaves — light color: interprets distance —
these leaves are blown farther away
Draw leaves with the speed of wind.

(1) Branch and stems — medium color
From bottom To top, just as bamboo grows.
Node with dark ink.

(2) Leaves — dark color
From bottom leaves to top leaves.

雨
竹
Bamboo in rain

Press here

Press here

Draw leaves with the feeling that
you yourself are in the rain, and
with the speed of falling rain.

鷺

Heron

Dark color for beaks, eyes, legs, and claws.
Medium color for outlines of bodies and color of beak.

(C)

(B)

(A)

After finishing heron in the order of (A), (B), (C), draw willow tree in two strokes

(A) SHORT WATERFALL

(1) Rocks — light color first
Dark color over light color
to show "wrinkles."
(2) Water — very light color
(3) Branch — medium color

Rocks where water falls are
a little darker than upper part.

滝
Waterfall

(B) LARGE WATERFALL

Ink only at tip of brush.

① ②

Rocks

Light color first.
Dark color outline next.

Maple
branch
last. For
leaves,
refer to
MAPLE.

罌粟

Poppy

Three different techniques for petals.
Apply ink only to half of brush.

ink WATER

(A) SLANTED BRUSH

Hold brush at
45° angle to
paper.

(C) ROLLING BRUSH

(B)
TOP TO BOTTOM

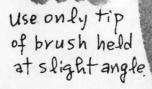

Use only tip
of brush held
at slight angle.

Hold brush as flat as possible,
and roll it from one side to the
other.

楓
maple

(1) Leaves — wet brush

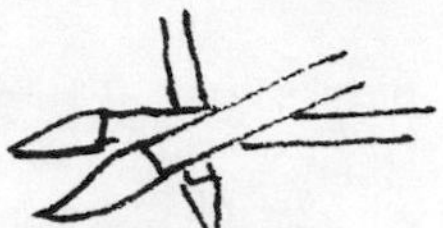

Press brush to form
each leaf.
Veins with dark color.

(2) Branch — from top to bottom
with dark color,
dry brush.

(1) Leaves —
wet brush

蔦
Ivy

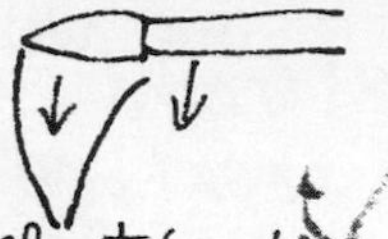

Slant brush.
Draw from
inside to
outside

(2) Vines —
from top
to bottom with
dark color, medium
moisture.

瓢簞

Gourd

Almost anything related to nature becomes a subject in Japanese painting—even this common gourd.

(1) Gourd — left-side outline first, right-side outline next, shading with wet brush, medium ink.

(2) Leaves with slanted brush. Draw top leaf first, then bottom leaf continuously without renewing ink, so that top leaf is darker.

(3) Vine—with moderate speed.

In this picture the tones of the ink have much to do with the final result.

The rooster is the symbol for rising early in the morning. Rising early is also a sign of industriousness.

雄鶏
Rooster

(1) Beak, eye, comb, and wattle

(3) Breast

(4) Wing

(5) Tail with dark color

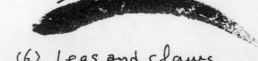

(2) Outline for neck and body

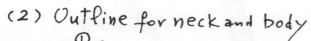

(6) Legs and claws

闘
鷄

Fighting-cock

Three poses
to choose from

(1) Beak, eye, comb,
and neck
Wattle is shown
by outline.

(2) Breast — dark-
color touches
over light-color
wash

(3) Wings

(4) Tail feathers

(5) Legs and
claws

(A) WET BRUSH

(C) MEDIUM MOISTURE

(B) DRY BRUSH

帆
船
Sail boat

(1) Sail first
Strokes are from left to right, top to bottom.

(2) Mast—from top to bottom

(3) Ropes

(4) Boat—from left to right.

If you draw land on the right side, as in (B), it will suggest that the boat is departing (for work). It also symbolizes the starting point in life or the beginning of a new enterprise.

Again, if you put the land on the left side of the boat, it will mean its homecoming or return.

The lobster is used as a New Year decoration and also for many other happy occasions. It is a symbol of long life — to live long until one's back is bent as the lobster's.

海老
Lobster

(1) Eyes, horns, and feelers

(2) Shell   Apply dark ink to half of brush, and press hard.

(3) Segments and tail
Dark ink on tip of brush; use slanted.

(4) Legs

(5) Short legs
One to each segment.

(1) Eyes and Shell
After applying medium-color ink thoroughly on brush, apply dark ink on tip.

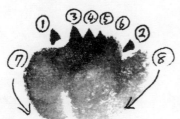

蟹
Crab

(2) Pincers — medium-color ink

(3) Legs
Darker medium color

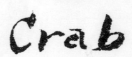
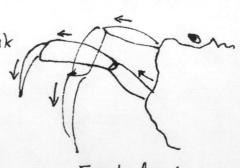

Each leg in one stroke, slightly pressing at each section.

(1) Eyes — dark-color ink

(2) Body in two pressed touches — dark color

(3) Wings

(4) Dark-color lines on wings and for claws.

(5) Grass Light color from bottom to top.

蝙蝠
Bat

鶴

Crane

The crane, together with the tortoise, is the symbol of long life.

(1) Beak ① → ② → ③ → Dark color

(2) Eye — Dark color

(3) Head and outline on left side — medium color

(4) Jaw and outline on right side — medium color

(5) Wings — medium color

(6) Tail feathers — dark color

(7) Legs and claws — from top to bottom with dark color.

(8) Reeds with medium color

For (3),(4),(5) hold brush straight up.

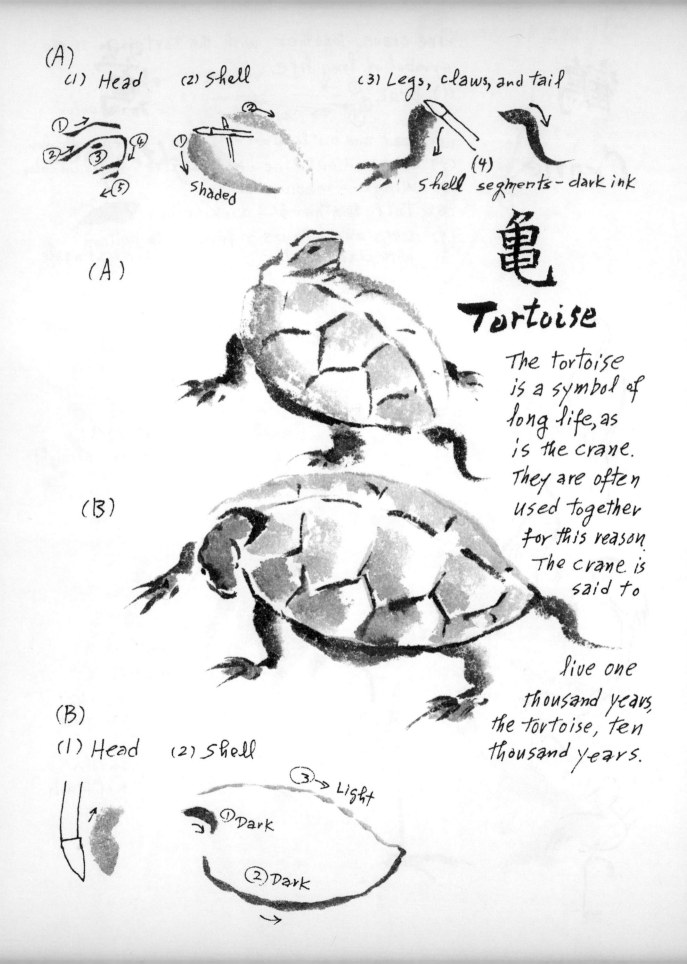

(A)
(1) Head   (2) Shell   (3) Legs, claws, and tail

① ② ③ ④ ⑤   ① ② Shaded   (4) Shell segments - dark ink

(A)

亀

Tortoise

The tortoise is a symbol of long life, as is the crane. They are often used together for this reason. The crane is said to

(B)

live one thousand years, the tortoise, ten thousand years.

(B)
(1) Head   (2) Shell

③ Light

① Dark

② Dark

鶯

Nightingale

(1) Nightingale
① —·— ·
② — ·—
③
④

(2) Plum trunk

outline of
snow-shaded

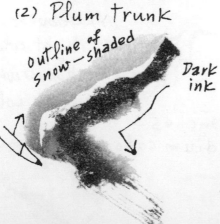

Dark
ink

(3) Branches
All from bottom
to top.
Brush straight up.

(4) Blossoms
Light color

(5) Outline of
snow-covered
roof

Medium color
on tip of brush.

Pomegranate

柘榴

(1) Wet brush
Apply dark ink on
half of brush.
Pomegranate shaped in
one stroke.

Twist your
hand as you
turn brush.

(2)

(3) Branches—
medium color

(4) Leaves—
light color.
Veins with
dark color.

栗
Chestnut

(3) Branch from top to bottom

(4) Leaves

(1) Ripe nut
Use brush flat, with ink only at the tip.

Needles with dark ink from inside to outside.

(2) Young nut

Dark ink at tip of brush. Brush vertical, circular motion. Spines last, with dark ink.

Veins with dark ink.

菊

Chrysanthemum

The chrysanthemum is the *Imperial Crest*.

(1) Flowers and bud
Use brush straight up.

(2) Stem.

(3) Leaves

老松
Old pine

(1) Pine needles—
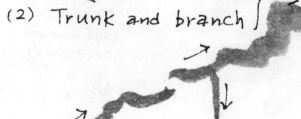
　　　　dark color

(2) Trunk and branch

(3) Stone wall
Medium color for outlines,
then light-color wash
all over.

(4) Castle
Medium color for
outlines, light
color on roof.

(5) Pine trees in
distance —
dark color

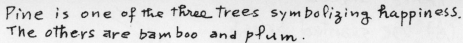

Pine is one of the three trees symbolizing happiness. The others are bamboo and plum.

松
Pine

Dark-color needles may be added to the pine below for this effect.

(1) Light-color touches with wet brush

(2) Trunk from bottom to top with light color

(3) Dark-color touches added over light color, starting from top of tree.

(4) Needles (not always necessary)

(5) Bark with medium-color dots (not always necessary)

Three styles

(A) Use slanted brush

Paper

(B) Use side of brush

Paper

(C) Draw outlines, fill

朝顔

Morning-glory

(A)

(B)

(C)

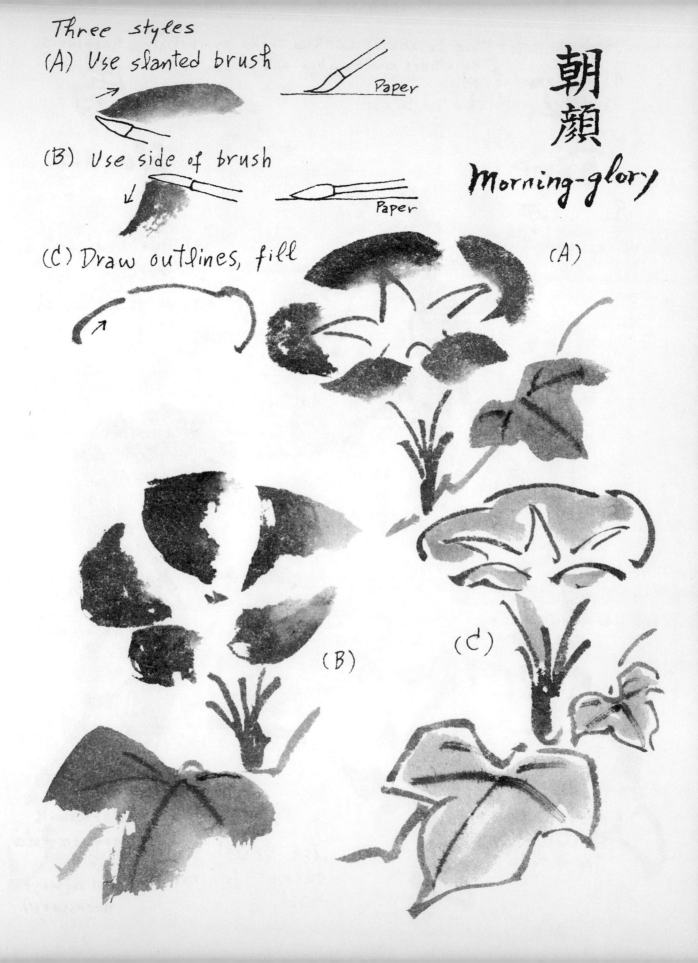

Medium color for body

(1) Ears and head
(2) Mane, with slanted brush
(3) Body

馬
Horse

(4) Tail like question mark
(5) Legs and hooves

Use brush straight up
except for mane and
tail.

孔雀
Peacock

(1) Beak, eye, jaw, head, crown, and neck

(2) Body and wings   (3) Breast and leg   (4) Feathers

(5) Peach tree

(1) Dark-color dots for stamen

(2) Petals — After applying light color thoroughly on brush, apply dark color on tip only. Use slanted brush. Do not renew ink until all petals are finished.
From inside petals to outside, in this order:

牡丹
Peony

(3) Leaves

Veins with dark ink.

(4) Stem from bottom to top, with medium color.

Hina Doll

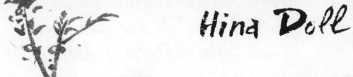

Hina or Ohinasama are the dolls which are displayed for the Girls' Festival on March 3rd each year.

(1) Outlines for both dolls with dark-color ink
(2) Pine trunk and cherry blossoms on costumes — dark ink
   Other parts — light or medium ink
(3) Peach branch — medium color, from bottom to top

It is the custom to use peach blossoms
with Hina Dolls.

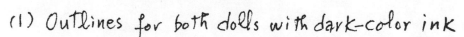

觀月
Moon viewing

The moon is a very popular subject in Japanese painting. It symbolizes purity of the heart. The moon always helps to give the feeling of stillness and solitude to the painting.

This picture is done mostly with lines and is one example of a simplified method of drawing human figures.

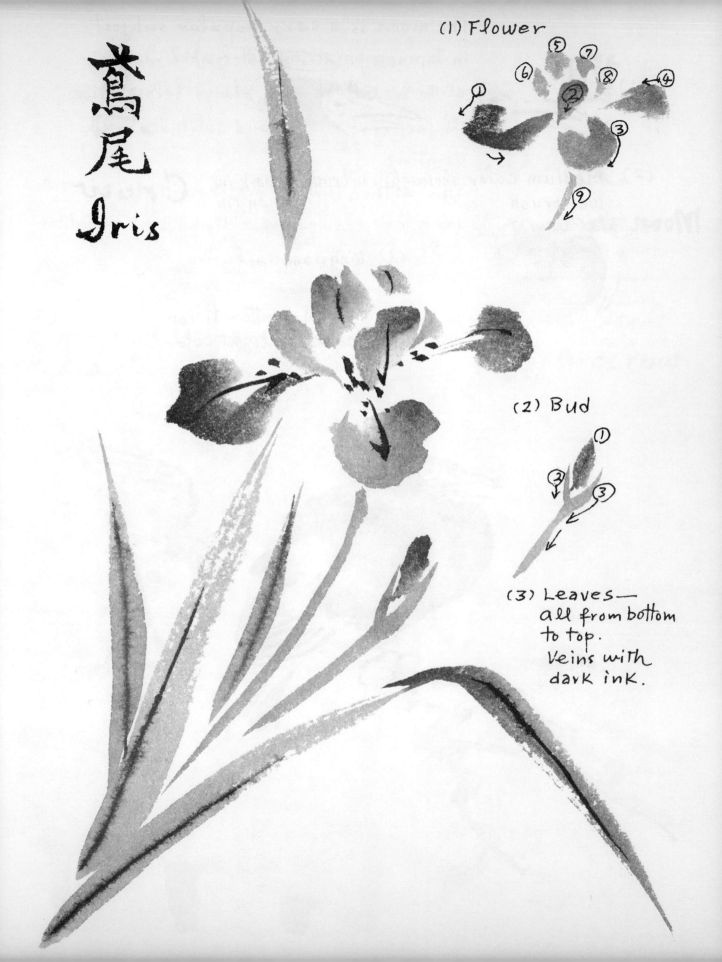

鳶尾
Iris

(1) Flower

(2) Bud

(3) Leaves—
all from bottom
to top.
Veins with
dark ink.

(1)

Crow

(2) Medium color thoroughly on brush, add dark ink on tip.
    wet brush

Body

(3) Wings and tail
(4) Claw
(5) Branch — bottom to top
(6) Leaves — light color

Dark color is used only for scarecrow.
All other parts are with medium and light color.

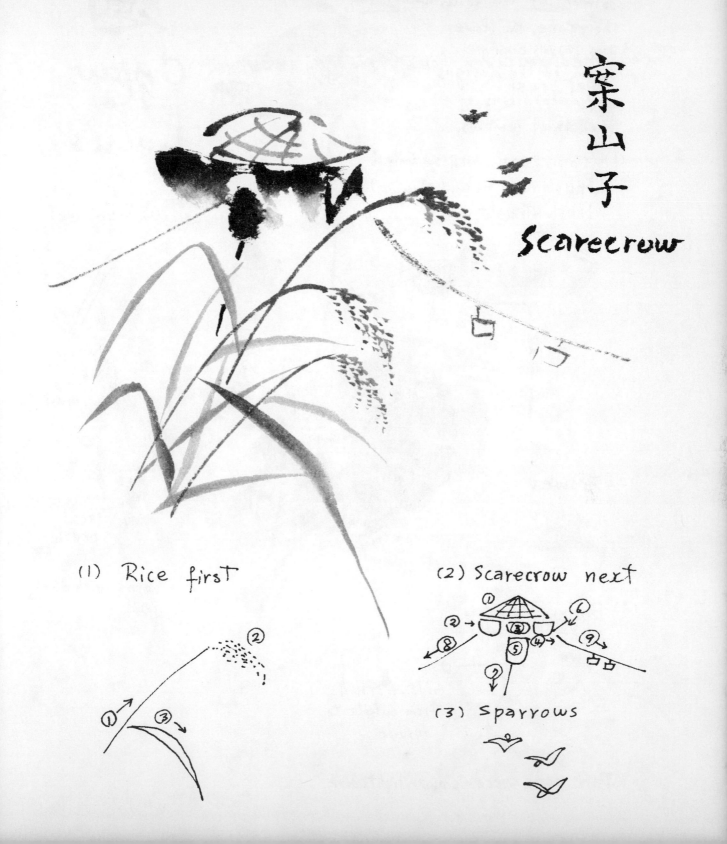

案山子
Scarecrow

(1) Rice first

(2) Scarecrow next

(3) Sparrows

The lotus is closely connected with Buddhism. Buddha is always shown seated on a pedestal formed by the lotus blossom. Therefore, the flower and leaves can be seen in the designs and decorations of Buddhist temples.

蓮
花
Lotus

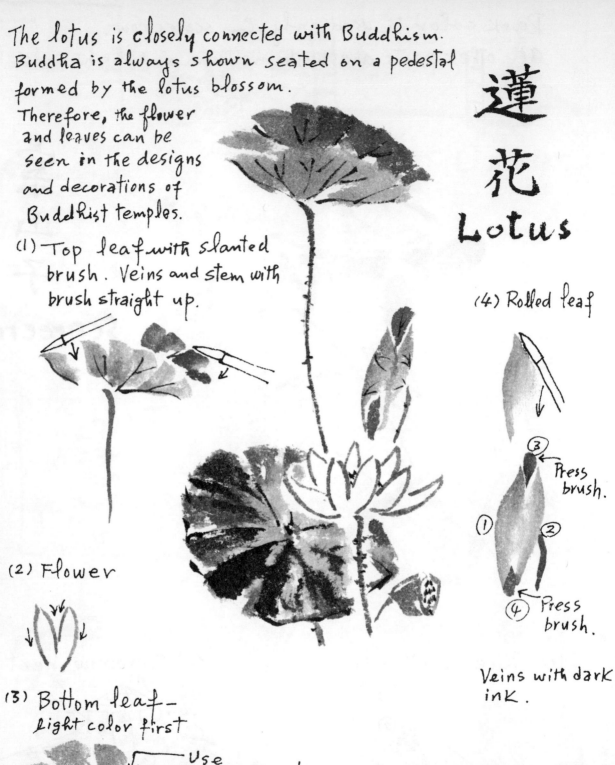

(1) Top leaf with slanted brush. Veins and stem with brush straight up.

(4) Rolled leaf

③ Press brush.

① ②

④ Press brush.

Veins with dark ink.

(2) Flower

(3) Bottom leaf— light color first

Use side of brush from outside to inside.

Dark color accents over light color.

Golden Gate Bridge

Washington D.C.

Mt. HOOD

Lake Washington

Salt Lake City

Chicago

NEW YORK

Larchmont, N.Y.

Milwaukee

From my sketch book

CHAPTER 8

MOUNTING AND DISPLAYING

BECAUSE VIRTUALLY ALL aspects of sumi e are unique, a final word concerning the mounting and displaying of brush paintings is in order. In Japan the sumi artist usually prefers to concentrate his efforts only on painting, and sends his work to a professional for mounting. These men are familiar with all the sumi surfaces—from rice paper to gold paper —and know their peculiarities. They know what can be done and what cannot be done with each surface. They know the type of "framing" that will do the most to enhance a particular subject or surface. In America only the larger cities offer professional mounting facilities, and unfortunately, few mounters are able to handle sumi paintings. Nevertheless, by exercising caution, anyone can mount his work and do a good job of it.

After a rice-paper painting has dried thoroughly, it will be crinkled and wavy. This is normal behavior for rice paper, and it does not mean the painting is ruined. Lay a sheet of white rice paper the same size as the painting (or slightly larger) on a clean, flat surface, and lay the painting face down next to it. Next, spray both sheets with clear water. Make up a smooth, *watery* wheat or flour paste; then, using a wide brush, spread paste evenly on both sheets. Carefully pick up the painting, holding it by two corners, and lay it paste-side down on the other sheet, beginning with one edge. Place a clean, dry sheet of paper—any kind of paper—on top of the painting, and with the hands rub thoroughly from the center out to the edges to remove air bubbles. If any small wrinkles show in the painting surface after rubbing, do not attempt to separate the pasted sheets or they will tear. Instead, cover them again with the dry paper, and pound it gently with the side of the fist. This will flatten the wrinkles and make them tiny enough so they will not be noticeable. Leave the pasted sheets flat until they dry, then trim the edges of the larger sheet. Remember, the sumi painting itself must always be completely dry *before* mounting.

Rice-paper and gold-paper paintings can also be pasted onto stiff white cardboard. A painting mounted on either rice paper or cardboard (or a shikishi painting) can, when dry, be pasted onto a larger colored mat or poster board, which will frame the light surface. The mat should be a dark, neutral tone, such as black or gray, to complement not the room furnishings, but the sumi painting. A glassed frame should not be used, since glass reflects light and gives the painted surface an artificiality, thus robbing the painting of its unique quality—its natural appearance. A painting can be mounted on a hanging vertical scroll, or a painting can be executed directly on the surface of scrolls made specially for this purpose.

Almost every home in Japan has a *tokonoma*, or alcove, whose purpose is displaying a single painting or a flower arrangement. The tokonoma is usually situated in a corner of the main room of the house and consists of a raised rectangular platform 6 feet long by 3 feet wide, with a wooden post at its outside corner that extends from floor to ceiling. A *kakemono* (scroll) is hung at eye level, and a square painting is hung slightly higher, just to one side of center in the tokonoma. The flower display is placed below and in front of the painting, also to one side. A painting and a flower arrangement are intended to complement each other. Thus, a sumi painting showing chrysanthemums would never be hung in conjunction with a display of real chrysanthemums. A sumi painting can, of course, be hung on a wall, but because of the simplicity of sumi e it should be alone on a wall and should not compete with other

pictures. More than one sumi painting can be displayed in a room, but they should not be hung in pairs. The aesthetic ideal for a room in a traditional Japanese home is a sumi scroll in the tokonoma, a calligraphy scroll on another wall, and a pair of painted (usually on gold) folding screens.

126

Not all American homes lend themselves to such Japanese ideals, nor is it always possible to change sumi paintings with the season of the year, as is the Japanese custom. However, in addition to those suggestions above which are suitable for American homes, there are some common-sense suggestions for display that will make a sumi painting more than just a decoration. If a painting is hung in a child's room or in a nursery, the subject should be appropriate for a child (carp, or kami bina). If a painting is hung in a guest room, it should, insofar as possible, be appropriate for any guest. A painting that has personal meaning or is symbolic for the immediate family would be out of place in a guest room. If a painting of a horse or a cat, for example, is hung in one of the main rooms of the house, and if a guest known to have a dislike for horses or cats is invited, such a painting might better be replaced or temporarily removed so the guest will feel at ease. Sumi e is an art of peacefulness, and serenity should be implicit from its conception to its display.